First Light

First Light

A Year of
Wisdom and Insight

Insight for Living

Charles R. Swindoll graduated in 1963 from Dallas Theological Seminary, where he now serves as the school's fourth president, helping to prepare a new generation of men and women for the ministry. Chuck has served in pastorates in three states: Massachusetts, Texas, and California, including almost twenty-three years at the First Evangelical Free Church in Fullerton, California. He is currently senior pastor of Stonebriar Community Church in Frisco, Texas, north of Dallas. His sermon messages have been aired over radio since 1979 as the *Insight for Living* broadcast. A best-selling author, he has written numerous books and booklets on many subjects.

Editor in Chief: Cynthia Swindoll
Application Writers: Jenni Key, Barb Peil, Christianne Varvel
Editor: Christianne Varvel
Graphic System Administrator: Bob Haskins
Director, Communications Division: John Norton
Print Production Manager: Don Bernstein
Print Buyer: Becki Sue Gómez

ISBN 1-57972-360-8
Cover design: Michael Standlee Design
Cover image:© Daryl Benson / Masterfile

Printed in the United States of America

Dear Friend of Insight for Living,

Twenty years may seem like a long time, but the past two decades at Insight for Living have felt like a brief few months at the most. One moment you're wearing a blue leisure suit, sitting with all your kids around the kitchen table; in what seems like the end of that season, you find your grandkids wearing polyester clothing as part of a retro culture flashback. It just doesn't seem possible.

But of course, it is. Twenty years is nothing to an eternal God and His ever relevant Word. After all, that prince of prophets, Isaiah, promised that the Word of our God would endure forever (Isaiah 40:8). You and I can be assured that the Bible will always be right on target, no matter the time or place.

That's why Insight for Living has committed all its efforts in the past twenty years to teaching God's Word accurately, clearly, and practically. Our all-time top priority has remained constant: to give you biblical truths that apply to your everyday life. In keeping with that goal throughout these twenty years, I've written monthly letters to the IFL listening family all around the world as encouragement for living the Christian life.

In your hand, you hold 365 excerpts from those two decades of letters—one thought for every day of the year, along with an insightful application of its teaching. Perhaps you'll remember when you first read some of these selections in years past. I hope that they will help you understand God's Word and His character more clearly as you enjoy a maturing, intimate, dynamic walk with Him.

This book has been designed for you to read quickly . . . at the same time, it offers a lifetime of application. As it reflects God's truth, invite its godly insight into your day at morning's first light or evening's end.

First and always committed to Him,

Charles R. Swindoll

January 1

A brand new year is here—let's start this one right! Determine to strengthen each day by investing a slice of time in quietness, prayer, and reading His truth. Let's turn these twelve months into the most diligent and determined months of asking and seeking and knocking we have ever pursued.

As this year begins, write out a prayer of commitment to your Lord and Savior. Seal it in an envelope and label it with today's date.

January 2

Who knows the challenges that await us? To underscore the reality of that question, consider another one: Who would have ever imagined this past year would have been as it was?

Reflect on God's goodness and provision of last year. Read Psalm 33.

January 3

When love is nurtured through the passing years, it becomes seasoned and enriched by the mixture of heartache and happiness. Is it easy? Not always. Are there adjustments? Many. But God faithfully reminds us that nothing should discount the commitments we make to our relationships.

Many of your greatest joys will come through your investment in key relationships. For whom will you commit to pray and nurture this year?

January 4

The foundational secret of scriptural insight is simple. It begins with a consistent reading of the Bible, not a random reading here and there. If you've been wondering how to get more personally involved in the Bible, you will accomplish that goal by reading through it consistently.

Find a Bible reading plan that complements your schedule and preferences. Make that time of reading and meditating on God's Word a priority.

JANUARY 5

If you are like me, you love fresh beginnings. There's nothing quite like the emotional rush of starting new projects or planning new ventures. Excitement is high, and motivation surges us onward.

What ministry project have you always wanted to pursue? Seek out an opportunity to serve others in your home, neighborhood, church, or mission field.

JANUARY 6

Most of us have great hindsight. Looking back, life becomes clear, uncomplicated, easy to explain. Who can't see things clearly once they've already occurred? Our greatest resource for facing the unknown without fear or frustration comes from our knowing and loving God.

Sketch out your life's spiritual journey on a timeline. What milestones, high points, and struggles have marked your journey?

January 7

To help us order our lives, God has provided us with bite-sized chunks of time called *days*. He even set aside one special day for us to rest, to think, and to appraise how well we have redeemed the time He has allotted us.

Reflect on Psalm 90. How can you "present to [God] a heart of wisdom" (v. 12)?

January 8

We cannot live on yesterday's provision, though hindsight assures us that God will provide. Nor do we have the foresight to know all the details ahead of time. Only He knows those things, and our trust in Him is firm.

What do you need God to provide today? Reflect on His faithful provision in times past to affirm your confidence in Him once again.

JANUARY 9

God's actions provide a model for us, a pattern worth following. He is pleased when we plan ahead, when we live lives full of purpose and meaning. Accomplishments done for His glory honor His name.

Before making any commitments or plans for this year, meditate on Psalm 16:1-3. Keep this verse in mind when planning your steps.

JANUARY 10

It is with renewed commitment that I step into this new year. I am encouraged to find others—you are probably among them—who are determined to make a difference these next twelve months. Tough times need strong-minded people to stand in the gap.

The Christian marathon is not a solo run; we depend on one another for strength. Who are you helping along and trusting for encouragement?

JANUARY 11

We often make excuses for mediocrity. Budget cuts, dead-lines, and hard-nosed practicality outshout and undermine excellence—even among God's people, who were once models of moral, ethical, and spiritual excellence. But Scripture exhorts us, "If there is any excellence and if anything worthy of praise, dwell on these things."

Memorize Philippians 4:8-9 this month.

JANUARY 12

The next time you feel trapped by winter's icy blast or chilling rain, read some of Scripture's great love chapters—Psalm 103, Romans 8, 1 John 4—and warm up to the blaze of God's unconditional, personal, unchanging love for you. It will be a breath of spring air in the middle of a long, cold winter.

Read the chapters listed above, and write a description of God's love for you. Refer to this description when life obscures your view.

January 13

How is it possible for those who don't know the future to walk into it with courage? That takes insight . . . a balanced blend of wisdom, vision, discernment, intuition, and anticipation.

Do you know someone who has walked with the Lord for many decades? Learn from their experiences and spiritual maturity.

January 14

Hopefully, this new year will be like none other in our lives. Even though we are sure to face unexpected tests, our God will prove Himself faithful. By His grace, we will learn and grow and mature as never before.

Are you confident that you will grow this year through unexpected tests? Read Philippians 1:3-6.

January 15

Developing insight is neither accidental nor incidental. By deliberately focusing on who God is, envisioning what He wants to accomplish, and drawing upon His power to make it happen, we gain the wisdom needed to face the unknown without frustration or fear.

The book of Proverbs teaches how to be wise in daily living. Read chapter 15 to discover how to use this wisdom when facing conflict.

January 16

A crucial step in knowing Christ is understanding and obeying His Word. May your heart be warmed as you draw into a deeper, more intimate relationship with the Lord Jesus—and anticipate some great discoveries ahead!

Does your church offer Bible study classes? Enroll today to learn how to accurately handle the "word of truth" (2 Timothy 2:15).

JANUARY 17

Every Christian was once a fugitive from grace. Only through Jesus' advocacy were we able to come home.

Somebody needs to receive God's grace through your actions today. Model God's love and grace to them in a tangible way.

JANUARY 18

In my weary moments, I wonder, "How can we handle more?" and "What's the secret to hope and victory in the midst of such enormous challenges?" It doesn't take long for me to answer: prayer.

When you feel discouraged or overwhelmed, pray. Read Psalm 116:1-2.

January 19

What God creates, God sustains. As the Scriptures state so
clearly, He upholds all things—*all things*—by His power.
The universe may seem fiercely independent, but it is
wholly dependent upon its Creator.

*Think the world is spinning out of control?
Read Colossians 1:16-17. Consider how He orchestrates
the events of your life for your good and His glory!*

January 20

To think that God is pleased to spread His glorious
message through us is almost more than I can fathom.
By His grace, we are used to change lives. What a tragedy
it would be to neglect this opportunity and allow the adversary an entrance into a calling as unique and strategic
as ours!

*Do you know someone in full-time ministry?
Write them an e-mail or letter, and ask
what you can do to encourage them.*

January 21

When confronting error, walk in love while embracing and expressing truth. Grace elevates godliness; it never cheapens it.

Ask God to turn confrontation into an opportunity for edification. Remember I Corinthians 8:1b: "Knowledge makes arrogant, but love edifies."

January 22

I want to challenge you to make this the year you grow deep in your Christian walk. Begin by concentrating on prayer. Pray diligently—daily—that God would open your mind and prepare your heart for the sowing of fresh seed from His Word.

Create a prayer list that details how you desire God to work in your heart. Thank Him for His continued work in your life.

January 23

Grind. Grind. Grind. Two things help relieve us from this threatening menace: an eternal perspective and a personal touch. The reminder that God's lovingkindness is "new every morning" gives us grace to cope with the grind, as does an arm around our shoulders or a kind word of encouragement.

Model the truth of Hebrews 10:24: "Let us consider how to stimulate one another to love and good deeds . . . [by] encouraging one another."

January 24

Pack five items in your suitcase for your trek across this new year: the desire to obey God, the willingness to be still, a faithfulness to commitments, an eternal perspective, and faith for the unknown. Package them securely for a lighter load on the journey.

Which of these five items do you need to instill in your life this year? How will you accomplish this goal?

January 25

I challenge you to trust God with every detail of your life, every dollar you spend, every decision you make from now until the end of the year. Embrace the challenge to be obedient to His leading.

Memorize Proverbs 3:5-6. Which of your ways does God desire you to entrust to Him right now?

January 26

Through prayer, God's grace, and our disciplined determination to stay at the task, we will get the job done. Did you catch that key word? Discipline—it's essential. You and I and every member of Christ's family must apply it to our lives each day.

How can you model God's grace and love in each conversation or passing comment you make today?

January 27

I have found that my trust and dependence on Him grow deeper when I meditate on Scripture. Paul underscores this idea in his letter to the Romans: "Oh, the depth of the riches both of the wisdom and knowledge of God!" (11:33).

Read Romans 12 to discover how to shine
the light of God's abiding wisdom in your life.

January 28

Each January brings renewed expectations for the year ahead, doesn't it? By this time next year, you will have grown through the inevitable challenges you'll face in the coming months. Look forward to a great year ahead!

The only thing that determines your growth from one year
to the next is God's action and your response.
Echo the response of Habakkuk 3:18-19.

January 29

Just as Abraham "went out, not knowing where he was going" (Hebrews 11:8), we are headed into the unknown future. This year, God will do things in your life that He's never done before. On the road ahead, renew your commitment to His truths daily.

What are your fears concerning the future? Learn from the faith warriors of Hebrews 11 — those saints who walked into the unknown with complete confidence.

January 30

Have you ever been struck by the enormity of a task and the vision that must have been required to complete it? It makes me realize the value of moving more slowly, thinking more deliberately, and living more thoughtfully. Speed may appear efficient on the surface, but it usually yields shallow relationships and a superficial walk with God.

Are you involved in a project that feels too pressing for a pause? Suspend action in order to think more clearly and plan more deliberately.

January 31

Prayer support acts like a foundation beneath a structure. Though essential, it is neither seen nor applauded—but it is the secret of stability.

Since no one except God can read your thoughts, you can be in private conversation with Him a thousand times each day. What do you want to tell Him right now?

February 1

God is not a fine old gentleman, standing back as a spectator of human events. His providence is far more than a reference to His foreknowledge.

God is intimately acquainted with all of our ways, but He also controls the world's leadership and events. Want proof? Read Proverbs 21:1.

FEBRUARY 2

"Discipline yourself for the purpose of godliness"
(1 Timothy 4:7). Paul challenged Timothy to rid himself
of every encumbrance, any needless habit, any weakening
tendencies that impeded the formation of godly character.
If we hope to excel, we must strip ourselves down to our
spiritual objectives.

Has your commitment to grow closer to God begun
to fade? It's never too late to begin again.
Renew your commitment today.

FEBRUARY 3

We need to take God's Word seriously. It is not to be
ignored, argued with, or questioned. His Word calls for
obedience.

What biblical command do you find difficult to obey?
Trust God to affirm each step,
no matter how small, in the right direction.

February 4

As winter drags on and excitement and enthusiasm wane in our lives, as we are tempted to toss in the towel and quit in discouragement, the apostle Paul's reminder to stay at it "in season and out of season" gives much-needed encouragement (2 Timothy 4:2).

In what season is your spiritual life right now?
Whether it's spring or winter, stand in
His service again today.

February 5

It's easier to stay at a tough task if we do it together. Be accountable to someone in your commitments to God and others day after day, week after week, month after month.

Take to heart the wisdom of Proverbs 27:17.
Find a partner to encourage you
on your spiritual journey.

February 6

God is sovereign. He is in full control, orchestrating every detail and sustaining us not only month to month but on a moment-by-moment basis. What comfort this brings as we "walk by faith, not by sight" (2 Corinthians 5:7).

Write Galatians 2:20 on an index card, and post it where you will see it often.

February 7

Some wise sage once said, "We are most like beasts when we kill. We are most like man when we judge. We are most like God when we forgive." His grace is our guide, His wisdom is our message, and His will is our goal.

Make a list of the struggles you faced in the last year. Ask for God's forgiveness, and thank Him for the opportunity to start fresh.

FEBRUARY 8

I am convinced that by advancing on our knees through every detail of our lives, we will see one obstacle after another removed, one need after another met, one opportunity after another fulfilled.

Ask God what He would like to accomplish in your spiritual life, family life, ministry, career, and finances. Pray diligently, and wait for His response.

FEBRUARY 9

Unburden your soul. I encourage you to spend a few hours outdoors. If you live near a wooded area, walk slowly and quietly among the trees. If a pond or lake is close enough to be enjoyed—even if part of it is frozen over—enjoy it. Sit still and listen.

Reflect on Psalm 46:10.

February 10

Since the predicted famine is inescapable and teachers who tickle ears are here to stay, the most intelligent way to counteract biblical and theological ignorance is to be different. Tighten your belt and dig into a systematic, consistent study of the Scriptures on your own.

A study Bible or a Bible commentary can reveal valuable details about God's Word. Use these Bible tools to discover different perspectives.

February 11

For marriages to grow and become increasingly more fulfilling, couples must take time, must communicate openly, must cultivate the joys of intimacy and the sharing of each other's secrets.

How might you be more open and trusting with your spouse in the year ahead? Find a safe and honest refuge in your relationship.

February 12

Jesus' model of love is the most substantial model to emulate. Love that endures is love that intercedes and sacrifices.

Jesus said, "Just as the Father has loved Me,
I have also loved you; abide in My love" (John 15:9).
Abiding means "live with."
How can you live with Jesus' love?

February 13

Communicating love is a real art. It takes thought, a measure of risk, and creativity—and to be done right, it takes a real investment. After all, you and I are following the best model around: our Lord Jesus Christ, the ultimate translation of love.

Meditate on I John 4:7-11.

February 14

Let me encourage you to enter your loved one's world. Whether it's Valentine's Day or any other day, speak his or her language. Come up with some creative ways to say, "I love you with my whole heart." Friendships need a similar vocabulary.

Do you know your loved one's love language?
Affirm your love for them today
in the way they need it most.

February 15

You may be experiencing difficult times, feeling as though God has sealed shut the storm windows and has blown away your hope and happiness. As the seasons change, we all need an extra urge toward faithfulness— especially if times have been difficult.

God will not allow you to be overwhelmed by your
circumstances. Read Isaiah 43:1-8.

February 16

God promises peace to those who lean on Him. That promised peace is translated *shalom, shalom*. In the Hebrew language, a term is repeated for emphasis. That means that God's peace is an unending security, a sense of uninterrupted rest and calmness. It doesn't come from us, but from God—when we lean on Him.

In what areas are you struggling to find peace?
Commit your fears to His care.

February 17

With unwavering determination, Paul refused to back down or look the other way. Whether accepted or not, he made known his confidence in God and his disapproval of wrong. Swimming against the current was the only way of life he knew.

Give others an abundance of grace, but do not fail to
"stimulate one another to love and good deeds."
Read Hebrews 10:19-25.

FEBRUARY 18

In our overpopulated, impersonal world, it is easy to underestimate the significance of one. Since when does size or volume dictate the agenda? Those things aren't always significant . . . God has always underscored individual involvement.

The next time you're in a crowd, gaze at others with spiritual eyes. Make it your natural response to remember, "Jesus loves that person."

FEBRUARY 19

What troubles you? A lack of deep satisfaction? A frantic schedule emerges when speed replaces depth and activities replace a meaningful walk with God. But as our activities decrease, our level of satisfaction increases.

You most need rest when pressures dictate your schedule. Block out a small pocket of time today to rest and pray.

February 20

Our God not only struck the spark that gave us life, He continues to prompt each heartbeat in every chest. And what He does for us as individuals, He does for the vast universe about us.

Listen to your heartbeat. Let each beat remind you of God's gift of life and your dependence on Him for your next breath.

February 21

Righteousness is no longer exalted and godliness is no longer modeled. We're experiencing a growing hostility to the values that were once revered. God's Word gives us the insight we need in these troubled times, and it gives us renewed hope to press on.

Read 2 Timothy 4:3-5. What challenge does Timothy extend for living in times like these?

February 22

I never cease being amazed and grateful for God's timeless Word. It meets our needs! That's why the changes in society's values do not alter our goals; they only make the meeting of them that much more important.

First Timothy 6:11 encourages you to "pursue righteousness, godliness, faith, love, perseverance and gentleness." Are you modeling these things in your life?

February 23

Tough times call for fun moments. The need to laugh, to get outside the tight radius of our own pressures for a fresh perspective is not simply a luxury—it's essential for survival.

Identify two or three fun activities to enjoy with others. Plan your activities now to ensure follow-through.

February 24

God's Word alone helps you handle the harsh realities in your life. There is a war going on for our souls, and the pain often borders on the unbearable. As we turn to God's life-giving Word and allow its practical truths to refresh us, it is amazing how He helps us go on.

Feeling stressed today? Feeling pulled in every direction? Romans 5:3-5 will bring you encouragement.

February 25

Our God loves it when we call on Him in our need. He comes to our rescue again and again when we do!

Read Psalm 34:6-8 aloud.

FEBRUARY 26

I refuse to be discouraged or downhearted. Day after day, I open the Book of books to come to terms with what God says about the evils of a spiritually bankrupt world. And then, day after day, I apply those very truths to the issues of our times.

When you read the newspaper or watch the evening news today, pray that God would be glorified in the events of each story.

FEBRUARY 27

It was Plato who wrote, "The unexamined life is not worth living." Self-examination may be a painful and exacting discipline, but it is essential if our pursuit is excellence.

Meditate on Psalm 139.

February 28

Remember when cars used to get stuck? Well, cars no longer get stuck, but people do. Nothing pleases me more than knowing that our Lord brought fresh hope and healing to someone in desperate need.

Echo David's prayer in Psalm 51:10:
"Create in me a clean heart, O God,
And renew a steadfast spirit within me."

March 1

The year is not even three months old, but the blahs are starting to set in! And if the whole truth could be told, you might be discovering that your spiritual hunger is not as acute as it once was. Instead of your early morning meetings with the Lord, you're starting to slip back into a formal, less personal relationship with Him.

If your commitment to spend time with the Father
is waning, don't be discouraged.
Pick up where you left off.

MARCH 2

For better or worse, we are always modeling our faith—
especially in the dailiness of life. No doubt, people are
watching our lives to discover how our relationship with
Christ makes a difference in the daily grind. Does that
give you pause, as it does me?

*Offer encouragement to unbelievers with the same love
that you give to the body of Christ. Be both specific
and genuine.*

MARCH 3

Let's pray that we will be a catalyst for real change in the
lives of those who need Christ. As we roll up our sleeves
and join in His efforts, our lives are dramatically changed
and enriched. May our Lord enable that to happen in
your life.

*Ask a neighbor for advice. Once they sense that
you are on their side, they may be more open to hearing
about God, who is also on their side.*

March 4

God's governing authority is limitless. From the greatest to the least, nothing ever happens beyond the scope of His sovereign power and providential care. He makes the rain to fall, the sun to burn brightly, and the stars to twinkle.

Are you trusting God with both the large and small worries in your life? Commit all of your cares to His control.

March 5

We were created in God's image. Like Him, we possess an inner spirit with which He can communicate and from which we can respond in worship, in songs of praise, and in unselfish acts of obedience.

In the car, shower, kitchen, or office, sing your favorite worship song to the Lord today as an act of private worship.

MARCH 6

Spontaneity is a wonderful trait. Without anyone pushing or demanding, those who are spontaneous see a need and act upon it . . . all on their own.

When a need presents itself to you today, be spontaneous.
Meet that need on your own and
with the Lord's enabling.

MARCH 7

It is easy to forget that God not only loves cheerful givers, He also blesses them. He demonstrates His grace on their behalf. Isn't that just like Him? As He does that for you, I hope you will remember what a faithful Lord you serve.

Read 2 Corinthians 9:7-8 for God's instructions
on giving and the benefits we receive when we
obediently give to Him.

March 8

I couldn't help but chuckle when I read this letter that a young child wrote to God:

> Jesus, you and me is tight.
>
> I luv you, Richard (aged 6)

How are you doing on becoming "tight" with God? How has your love for the Lord increased over the years you've walked with Him?

March 9

I remember when I learned how to study the Bible for myself. What a change it made in my attitude, my marriage . . . my life. Imagine what would happen if all God's people knew the necessary techniques and principles to cultivate their own spiritual nourishment. Wow!

Begin the heritage early. Share with a child how a Bible verse helped you in a real-life situation.

March 10

Remove three words from your vocabulary: *chance, fate,* and *luck.* Those humanistic terms suggest that there are blind, impersonal, and spontaneous forces at work in the ranks of humanity. But only One is at work, and that One is God.

Are you attributing the circumstances of your life to random chance? Read Philippians 2:13.

March 11

We are partners in no minor project! Do you know why? Because there are lives at stake, and each one is of inestimable value to the Lord God.

A college campus is a great place to meet students from other countries, many of which will welcome your friendship and hospitality.

March 12

Our commitment to serve God with our lives makes a severe dent in the devil's plans. Instead of hopeless, the future is bright when we continue to reach out to the lost and spiritually needy. Won't you dedicate yourself to pray for them in these challenging times?

Prayer is not preparation for the battle; it is the battle. Partake in the battle by praying specifically and with enormous faith.

March 13

How do you adopt a deep assurance of faith? I know of only one way: by wrapping your hope and trust together in the certainty of God's character. The reminders of His unchanging character will keep you secure until you feel the warmth of His embrace once again.

Claim the promises about God's character described in Psalm 103. Thank Him for each attribute, one verse at a time.

March 14

It's easy to forget just how big and varied this world really is; we tend to view life from our own backyard. But He has commissioned us to get involved in the world for whom His Son died—a world of people who are often busy and active, yet lonely and desperate and lost.

*Smile and speak a word of kindness
to a stranger today — and every day.*

March 15

No one but God can change our lives. Only He can help us align our priorities, remain committed to our purity, and keep a check on our attitudes. As our hearts change, we discover the invitation to join His work.

*What one thing — large or small — is harming your
attitude or personal purity and needs to be
surrendered to God today?*

MARCH 16

Without exception, givers are grateful people. They are delighted to be a part of something they believe in, and that kind of attitude spreads infectious cheer.

Nursing homes offer great opportunities for personal outreach. As you cheerfully give of your time and attention, ask God to bless others through you.

MARCH 17

God is still in charge of this old earth. He specializes in impossibilities. What looks bleak and foreboding today can become beautiful and encouraging tomorrow— because His plan is not only good, it's **great**.

The last book in the Bible describes God's plan to make all things new (Revelation 21:5). Consider the joy of an eternity with Him.

MARCH 18

In times of grief, remember this: Though the sting of
separation is painful, death's curse no longer has power
over the Christian. In fact, death becomes the gateway
to heaven.

For comfort and assurance, read 2 Corinthians 5:8-9.

MARCH 19

It's hard to remember our true purpose when our schedules pick up speed and our compassion, patience, and joy
diminish at a corresponding rate. Intense schedules over-
whelm us when all we really need is to focus on God's
perspective, understand and obey His plan, and sense His
presence.

*Godliness never happens automatically. Make time
to be quiet and alone with your heavenly Father today.*

March 20

It really does take a certain amount of maturity and unselfishness to recognize a need and then take the initiative to make a difference.

What need do you see in your family, church, or neighborhood? Take the initiative, and ask how you can contribute.

March 21

Have you ever thought about how often Scripture mentions the seasons? Frankly, I was surprised when I checked—over sixty times! Our Lord is constantly at work. With divine skill, He paints the landscape a new color, melts the snow high above us, and fills our lakes and rivers anew.

What can you celebrate about this time of your life?

March 22

The primary object of our dependence is the Lord God. He uses His Word to convict, to bless, and to change lives. If we remove His hand from our lives, there is no way we could continue on. We rely on Him for our existence.

In what ways are you hesitant to depend on God? Commit these concerns to Him in faith.

March 23

Why does God prefer that we give rather than receive? Giving cultivates selflessness in us. It keeps us from becoming too attached to material things. It models the life Christ lived.

What do you have that another might need? Let your giving be a response to what Christ has given to you.

March 24

We are humbled when God uses us. No doubt Moses was overwhelmed when the Lord directed Him to lead the Exodus. And the prophets Isaiah and Jeremiah must have been stunned when He chose them as His messengers. He makes us His instruments to model His grace.

Know someone needing encouragement and life direction? Send them a note on which you've written Colossians 1:9-12.

March 25

In this day of ingratitude, it is rare to find folks with humble hearts overflowing with joy for all God has done. May this day find you full of gratitude that results in a heart full of joy.

*What are you thankful for today?
Reflect on God's goodness . . . praise Him
for His faithfulness.*

March 26

In any season, relaxation has little to do with our outward position and everything to do with our heart's posture before the Lord. When the heat rises and the wind blows, God always invites us to trust, delight, commit, rest. Rest beneath the cool branches of His sheltering tree.

Meditate on Psalm 37:1-7a.

March 27

We depend on others for encouragement. We are strengthened in our spirit to press on when we receive words of hope and acts of kindness from God's people.

The new person at your church is probably looking for fellowship. What kind word or gesture could you give to communicate care and acceptance?

March 28

We must apply insight to our lives, which tells us we should plan wisely, make our needs known to God and those around us, and then move ahead in faith as God provides what we need.

Memorize the words of Psalm 37:23.

March 29

A knowledge of the holy adds substance to our faith. An understanding of God's truth stabilizes us during times of testing. A comprehensive grasp of doctrine enables us to handle the Bible accurately. And in all things, growing in truth leads to a life of greater obedience and deeper joy.

Ask your pastor or Christian bookstore manager for a practical study of God's character, the Trinity, the end times, or another doctrinal issue.

March 30

My prayer is that for a few minutes each day, you will always find the kind of refreshment that you need. May the breeze of hope and the green pastures of God's Word quiet the stresses of your day and remind you of His endless grace and love.

Take a mini-vacation today. Take a walk, read some Scripture, listen to music — redirect your focus on God's goodness.

March 31

Because we do not know what tomorrow holds, we are forced to depend on the One who does. When we model such a walk, the Lord grants us the confidence we need to handle tomorrow without the anchor of anxiety weighing us down.

Want an antidote for future anxiety? Apply the words of Matthew 6:30-34 to your life.

April 1

My mentor and friend Howie Hendricks challenged me, saying, "Every time you impact the spiritual life of another individual, you set in motion a process that ideally never ends." They, in turn, have something to offer someone else.

Being a mentor is another way of being a friend. Though your ages differ, you can walk alongside your younger friend and simply point the way.

April 2

Perhaps you have discovered, as I have, that the only place of lasting peace is beside the Shepherd. The psalmist's words are a fitting reminder: "Though I walk through the valley of the shadow of death, I fear no evil, for You are with me" (Psalm 23:4).

When was the last time you thoughtfully read Psalm 23? Return to it again for renewed peace.

April 3

He heals me. Three simple words, but they couldn't be more profound. Healing is God's unique specialty—His exclusive prerogative. I have seen Him do what no one else could. Haven't you? And when He does, we appropriately stand awestruck and give Him our praise.

Who could use God's healing touch in your life today?
Surrender them to God's hand, trusting that
He works all things together for good.

April 4

God not only numbers the hairs on our heads, He determines the days of our lives. In doing so, He weaves everything together into His design. Ultimately, the tapestry of His handiwork will be something to behold!

From your perspective today, you see only the underside
of that tapestry. How might the tapestry of your life
look from a heavenly perspective?

April 5

People need each other. That doesn't discount the obvious truth that we desperately need God, but it does demonstrate God's plan that we model His character to each other.

What is your favorite attribute of God's character — love, joy, faithfulness, wisdom, strength? Who do you know that models that characteristic? Tell them so today!

April 6

Do you remember what it's like to be in a valley? Where did you go for help in those times? In His own inscrutable way, God uses His Word to remind us that no valley is too dark for the light of His truth.

Return to Psalm 23. Read the familiar Psalm in a not-so-familiar translation. What new meaning do you gain from it?

April 7

We tend to rush here and there, putting out fires rather than making the most of our time, as we are instructed to do in Ephesians 5:16. How great is our need for balance! Woven into the fabric of that word are the essential threads of wisdom, discipline, self-control, discernment, and insight.

Meditate on Ephesians 5:15-16.

April 8

While in captivity in Egypt, God's faithful people obeyed His command to sprinkle blood on their doorposts. In His faithfulness, God delivered them out of slavery's grip and sent them off for the Promised Land. It's that dramatic rescue that we celebrate at Passover.

Read the details of the event in Exodus 8-12. What value does God place on obedience to His Word? In what area of obedience do you pray for strength today?

April 9

How is your vision? When we reach into the homes and hearts of people beyond our comfortable circle, our breadth of vision expands and paves the way for the broadening of ministry.

In what kind of ministry would you love to play a part? Dream a little. How could you contribute to that ministry right now?

April 10

When Christ was only hours removed from the cross, He stood before the Father with integrity. He hadn't done what everyone else wanted Him to do or expected Him to do, but He had done everything the Father had sent Him to do . . . and in the final analysis, that's what mattered.

Early in His ministry, Jesus described His goal, which was ultimately accomplished in the Cross. Read John 4:34.

April 11

Do you realize that Christ prayed for us? He loved us enough to intercede for us, even though we did not come along until centuries later. Our believing in Christ is the direct result of His prayer for us that dark, difficult night before He was lifted up to die.

Meditate on John 17.
Do you understand how much Jesus loves you?

April 12

I can't help but marvel at how much Christ gave. He gave up heaven. He relinquished His will to follow the Father's directions. He poured Himself into His disciples. He gave Himself to the cross, with all of its humiliation. No wonder we love Him so!

To enhance your Easter celebration,
read Philippians 2:1-11.

April 13

I wonder at times if we fully grasp the gift Jesus gave us that weekend in Jerusalem—He endured the agony of Gethsemane and the isolation of Calvary. He loved us unto death.

Ponder Jesus' last night in the Garden of Gethsemane. Read Matthew 26:36-56.

April 14

Nothing can surpass God's love-gift at Calvary. And what a glorious remembrance it is when the saints of God pause, ponder, celebrate, and worship the resurrected Jesus.

Remember Christ's resurrection, your hope of glory. Read Luke 24.

April 15

Can I remind you today that the Resurrection is the most fantastic example of hope? When Christ rose from the dead, we were given hope—hope of forgiveness, hope of eternal life, and even hope for today and this very minute. That's reason for a yearlong celebration of Jesus' victory over death!

Consider Jesus' words in John 11:25-26.
Who needs to hear these words and be asked,
"Do you believe this?"

April 16

All through the Scriptures, money is seen as mere mammon—temporal, perishable, uncertain. When it is used for spiritual purposes, however, everything changes. He promises rewards for those investments because they add eternal dimensions to the use of our resources.

The saints described in 2 Corinthians 8:3-4 begged to contribute to God's work. What ministry in your local church can you financially support, even in a small way?

April 17

Christ's love knew no bounds, never wore thin, never reached the end of its tether. Instead, He prayed for His disciples again and again. Only hours before cruel hands seized Him and tortured Him, He drew near to the Father on behalf of His disciples.

His love for you also knows no bounds.
Meditate on Romans 8:38-39.

April 18

Let's recommit ourselves to one of the qualities that make for greatness—gratitude. Regardless of our present circumstances, we may still find numerous reasons to look upward with a smile and say, "Lord, how good You have been to me!"

Never fall asleep at night without thanking God for
something He did for you that day.

April 19

While money is important, focusing our full attention on finances is counterproductive. In fact, it is an exercise in futility.

Read what Solomon, the richest man in his day, said about money in Proverbs 23:5.

April 20

Contrary to popular opinion, vision, determination, and dreams are not reserved exclusively for the young. Let's dare to dream about today's potential and be ready to climb the mountain of tomorrow's fresh challenges!

What older person do you know who welcomes tomorrow's challenges? Ask them their secret.

April 21

I'm thankful that physical presence is not a prerequisite for personal relationship—especially when it comes to Christ.

Get a glimpse of the joy Peter described in I Peter I:8.

April 22

David could not have sustained his role as king of Israel without the support of many who believed in him and remained loyal to his leadership. We, too, need the support of each other as we participate in God's ever-expanding kingdom.

Make time in your day today to call, write, e-mail, or visit with a brother or sister in Christ. Make it your mission to encourage them in their walk with God.

April 23

Providence enlarges perspective, and all of us certainly need that—especially when so much of what we can see around us falls into the category of wickedness and wrongdoing.

Discouraged by the decline of righteousness in our world? Be certain, God is not done with this generation yet. Thank Him for His justice and faithfulness.

April 24

God desires our faith more than He desires our energy, our prayers more than our creativity, and our dependence on Him more than our ingenuity. Yet in His grace, He multiples them all.

Meditate on 2 Corinthians 9:8b: "And God is able to make all grace abound to you, so that . . . you may have an abundance for every good deed."

April 25

We must look to God for the provision of our needs. We need only trust Him to move as we present our needs before Him.

Read more of King Solomon's financial advice in Proverbs 23:4-5a.

April 26

I want to pass along a challenge. Get involved in an authentic "life-on-life" relationship with another person. Find out their needs, their hopes, and their God-given talents and abilities. Pray for their needs, and encourage them as God works in their life.

Model the truth of Ecclesiastes 4:9-10.

April 27

Partnership within the body of Christ is essential. It assures us that we're not alone, slugging it out on a deserted island. When partners surround us, staying at the task is found to be much easier.

Spending a lot of late nights working hard on a ministry project? Consider how you can invite someone to share in that privilege.

April 28

May our faithful, never-forgetful Lord give you peace of mind when you obey His prompting, and may you have the reassurance of heart that comes from being committed to eternal values.

What is God's guarantee for peace in Isaiah 26:3?

April 29

In our day of indifference, more and more people want
something for nothing, privileges without responsibility,
receiving without giving. Thankfully, we've received the
gift of grace—unmerited favor—that prompts us to be
stewards of that grace to our world as well. We give back
. . . because He gave.

Memorize I John 4:19:
"We love, because He first loved us."

April 30

We're not running this race alone—we're connected.
Encouragement within the body of Christ gives new
energy and motivation for the race set before us. Keep
shouting your encouragement, and drink deeply from
the wellspring of encouragement that filters toward you
from others.

*Aren't you glad you don't run this race alone? Thank
God for at least three people on whom you can call for
help or encouragement. Who can call on you?*

May 1

The psalmist was right—our times are in God's hands. And that's all the more reason to make each day count. Ask Him to show you where you can broaden your vision and determination to the greater glory of God. He will—I can assure you, He will!

Are you in God's waiting room?
Memorize Psalm 31:5, and repeat it back
to God when you feel anxious.

May 2

Like wisdom, learning to live by grace comes slowly. God is in no hurry as He purges graceless characteristics from us. But He is persistent. He is constantly working to transform us into the image of His Son, through whom grace and truth were revealed.

A diversity of books and topics are sure to keep you
growing. Resist the temptation to read only those books
that reinforce what you already know.

May 3

Again and again, Christ met those who felt worthless, abused, discouraged, and forgotten and refused to push them down with shameful words of condemnation. He continually lifted their spirits and helped them climb higher. With a fresh burst of honor, they believed they would become everything they were meant to be.

Do you believe you will become all that you are meant to be? Receive the unconditional acceptance Christ offers you today — and live with confidence!

May 4

If you find your hope wearing a little thin and have started to wonder how you can survive what's been thrown at you, remember this: **God is in control.** He's in control when the checking account is full and your health is fine—and He's also in control when life is dry and times are hard.

What are you trusting God for today? Share your confidence with someone whose faith is faltering.

May 5

Whatever God is doing in your heart comes from your willingness to embrace His truth. I want to encourage you today to let Him do His work. Welcome it, even when it's tough. You'll be so glad you did.

As you desire God to work in your life, He will faithfully complete everything He has in mind for you. Read Philippians 1:6 as a reminder of this promise.

May 6

Those of us who desire to walk with Christ need encouragement from fellow believers to lead holy, upright lives in the eyes of God, our families, and the world. We need endurance for the long haul, or as one author put it, "a long obedience in the same direction."

Just as somebody needs you for support, you need them. The Christian life is not supposed to be lived alone. Receive encouragement today . . . and give it away!

May 7

The great mystery you read about so often in Romans 8—
that "God causes all things to work together for good to
those who love God"—ends by stating that He desires us
to be conformed to the Son. As God works in our lives,
He chips away anything that doesn't look like Christ.

*How is God sculpting you to look more like
His Son? Be grateful that He smoothes out
our rough edges.*

May 8

It doesn't take long to see the tremendous priority God
places on relationships. Relationships blossom when both
parties are willing to be vulnerable, teachable, honest,
generous, and available.

*Our relationships with others testify that we are living
letters, "written in . . . hearts, known and
read by all men" (2 Corinthians 3:2).
What does your letter say today?*

May 9

Because of your commitment to Him, God continues to use you to change lives. As His hope, His riches, and His greatness are proclaimed, lives are changed. How wonderful it is to be a part of God's eternal plan!

Ever want to start a conversation about spiritual things but don't know where to begin? Rehearse open-ended questions, such as, "What do you think about God?"

May 10

We were amazed at the grace that came from believing in Christ, but think how necessary it is to demonstrate that same grace in our lives. Let's make it our goal to model grace.

You know what saving grace is; today, practice living grace. Shower it on every person you meet in the form of kindness, patience, love, and mercy.

May 11

God places His hand on your life to feel His Son's heart beating in you. He smiles when your heart beats after the things of God. His life in you, your hope of glory, is the celebration of the Christian life.

Do you know someone who has matured in Christ? Tell them that their faith is evident, and commit to support their continued growth by praying for them.

May 12

There is a bond deep within that binds us to one another. It is the glue of authentic love, expressing itself in compassion, fairness, supportiveness, and the aiding of another. Personally. Without strings attached.

The apostle Paul prayed that believers would be "encouraged, having been knit together in love" (Colossians 2:2). How can you knit warmth into someone's day?

May 13

Almost without exception, children embrace the truth because their parents modeled it. I have found that most of the great men and women who shaped history for the cause of Christ cultivated their appetite for spiritual things in a home where the mother or dad—often both—kept close to God's majesty.

Obey Proverbs 31:28 — call your mother.
You will bless her day.

May 14

Know that He will be faithful to strengthen you in your walk and prosper you in your way when you commit your heart and your deeds to Him alone.

Psalm 37:1-7 offers a great four-step walking plan
with God. Follow it to find peace and rest.

May 15

God is for us, not against us. He accepts us and surrounds us with protection and security. We are safe in His arms. If we remember that each morning and live in the light of it each day, what a difference it will make!

How does Romans 8:31-32 apply to you today?

May 16

Bible study and a few quiet moments in prayer lead to a growing intimacy with God. Set your heart to practice the insights you gain from your study. Be quick to apply the things that will strengthen your devotion to Him. Wherever God's Word takes root, lives are changed.

What have you read in God's Word recently that penetrated your heart? Ask God to quicken your heart to obey His specific Word today.

May 17

If the Christian life were a sprint—fast, hot, and over real quick—it'd be a snap. But it's not. It's a marathon, with enough uphill challenges that even the most dedicated become tempted to slow down or quit. That's why Scripture so often encourages us not to grow fainthearted or weary of doing what is right.

Allow the words of Hebrews 12:1b-2a to sink into your heart so that you may know how to endure your trials.

May 18

How is it in your home? When was the last time you shared something humorous, fun, or even something that warmed your heart? If you can't remember, it's time for a change—it's time to make joy a priority. Joy is not something you do; it's an attitude you choose to adopt.

What can you do to bring joy to your home? Share family stories, play a game together, or start a new tradition — make joy a family trademark!

May 19

God loves you. He smiles at the thought of you. You are the object of His attention and His affection. Nothing you do can make Him love you less . . . or more. His is an unchanging, unconditional love because it's based on His character, not ours.

God says, "I have loved you with an everlasting love; Therefore I have drawn you with lovingkindness" (Jeremiah 31:3). How have you seen Him do this in your life?

May 20

Someday we'll toss our track shoes next to the heavenly gates, and no matter how arduous or off-course our journey was at times, we'll rush headlong into our Savior's embrace. "Welcome home, child," He'll say.

If you have any doubts about your eternal destiny, talk to your pastor. You can be completely confident in the Bible's promises about your eternal home.

May 21

When we abide, we declare our dependence on the Lord. We need what only He can provide. We trust Him to nourish us, to care for us, to nurture us, and to protect us. And how does He do that? He often does it through our relationships with others.

Jesus' words in John 15:1-11 encourage you with God's promises when you abide in Him. Count His promises, and it'll add up to joy!

May 22

I've always liked this definition: "Joy is the flag that flies over the castle of the heart, announcing that the King is in residence today." When God is reigning in our hearts, His presence is reflected in our attitudes. Let that flag fly high!

Memorize Psalm 16:11 in the translation of your choice.

May 23

Interestingly, it often takes work to relax. It means letting go of yesterday's regrets and releasing tomorrow's agenda. Relaxation's telltale signs—a natural laugh, quieter thoughts, and easier breathing—reflect an attitude of calmness and trust.

To rest, you must relinquish control. What have you been holding too close that should be surrendered to God? What's keeping you from giving it to God right now?

May 24

If the truth were known, most of us use prayer like a fire escape: only in case of an emergency. But that's not the kind of prayer God encourages. He wants to engage you in natural, daily conversation.

When was the last time you called on God for a chat? He's waiting for you to enter His presence right now. Because of Jesus, you can approach Him at any time.

May 25

God's Word is sweet to me. Why? Because it has led me into a deeper intimacy with Him. Hopefully, you have that same passion for God and devotion to His Word.

How has God's Word led you to a deeper understanding of His character?

May 26

What do people really need or want? In a word, hope. Most folks I know are hungry for it, searching for it. Even Christians need the hope that grace affords. They need to know how to walk in a right relationship with God, through faith in Jesus Christ.

If you know someone who struggles with depression, hold out a word of hope to them. Tangibly show them that God is faithfully working behind the scenes.

May 27

The English poet Tennyson observed, "More things are wrought by prayer than this world dreams of." I am convinced that most things that happen in God's world can be attributed to the prayers of His people.

Pick a national, international, or missionary concern, and commit to pray for it throughout the next month.

May 28

Think about your relationship with God throughout the day. Keep a running dialogue with Him in prayer. Include Him in both the major and minor events of your day— He cares about them all.

Allow the words of I Peter 5:6-7 to decrease your stress level.

May 29

Use these questions to evaluate your grace quotient:
- Do I encourage, build up, and affirm those around me with my actions and words?
- Do I give the people I love the freedom to be who they are?
- Do people feel comfortable in my presence rather than intimidated?

Ask God to give you an opportunity to increase your grace quotient this week.

May 30

No matter my age, I can never get over that moment when I knelt at the cross. Think back to that hinge point in your own life . . . and never forget it.

Prepare a five-minute testimony that includes how you came to Christ and some recent evidence of His grace in your life. Be ready to share God's gift upon request.

May 31

Our love for God and His truth cannot be translated into a procedure that is merely operational and mechanical. That is not how God commands us to live our lives. Instead, our love for God prompts us to proclaim His truth and grace to the world.

Have Bible studies or church activities become a routine? Look and pray for a fresh way to enjoy God's people and His Word. Creativity is God-given!

June 1

Whether it is encouragement and comfort or nourishment and hope, a well-timed warning or a quiet word of reassurance, my prayer is that your every encounter with God's Word will meet that specific need in your life. May you be a sensitive and diligent student.

Being a student involves studying. If you have not yet made the regular study of God's Word a priority, now is a good time to begin.

JUNE 2

Aren't we strange creatures? Given a little relief in our schedules, we pack in more than normal, leaving ourselves somewhere between weary and exhausted. A hurry-up summer often leads to a frantic fall . . . and somewhere in the midst of the relentless pressure, our time alone with God gets the squeeze.

After six days of creation, God rested. Perhaps He did this so as to model rest for us. Why might God consider rest important?

JUNE 3

Five words faithfully linger in my mind: "That I may know [Christ]" (Philippians 3:10). Just think about that for a moment. Like Paul, we can make it our determined purpose to know Christ. Incredible.

How can you purpose to know Christ even more by the end of today? Through a lunchtime of prayer? A quiet time of reading His Word?

June 4

Our Savior undergirds our passionate pursuit to be deeply and intimately acquainted with Him. He patiently draws us to Himself, tugging at the hidden cords of our heart. And in that mysterious dance between His lead and our response, God reveals Himself to us.

Read John 1:14. Think about the love that prompted Christ's coming as a man.

June 5

As we dive deeper in our pursuit of knowing Christ more intimately, may we love Him more deeply, listen more closely, and follow more obediently than ever.

Consider the old refrain: "To see Thee more clearly, love Thee more dearly, follow Thee more nearly, day by day." Make that your song today.

JUNE 6

Spiritual erosion is a silent enemy. The Lord Jesus Christ, God's Son and your Savior, deserves your allegiance and seeks your worship. Don't let doubts or self-reliance creep into your relationship with God.

Allow the truth of Ephesians 2:8-9 to wash over you. Meditate on what it means to be saved by grace alone.

JUNE 7

I once observed a Texas sunrise where the clouds, tinged in pink, rolled quickly across the sky. Their gold-trimmed edges hinted at the sun below the horizon. When I see such a gorgeous sight, I can't help but grow anxious for the Lord to appear in those same clouds to draw His bride home with Him.

Read Revelation 14:1-7. Read through it slowly, and paint the picture in your mind.

JUNE 8

Grace is not something to be claimed only. It should be demonstrated—shared in friendships and drawn upon to sustain relationships. Grace-oriented generosity comes from the overflow of a liberated heart.

Someone in your daily circle may need to receive grace today. Be on the alert for an opportunity to extend it, and thank God for the daily measure He gives you.

JUNE 9

Many people around the world haven't found true joy because they don't know the Savior. And some people who do know Him don't know how to appropriate His grace into their lives. Communicate to others the joy that is discovered when we allow Him to reign as the sovereign King of our lives.

Will you summon your courage and share your faith with another today? Pray . . . go forth. The Holy Spirit will be your ally.

June 10

Here's an idea. Spend the summer immersing yourself in a small book of the Bible. Read through it once a week, memorize key passages, do word studies, get to know its background and author. Let this summer be one to remember in God's Word.

Consider the book of James — full of practical application. Or Philippians — full of godly exhortation. The list goes on . . . pick one and begin.

June 11

Once we've tasted a deep, intimate relationship with God, we are no longer satisfied with the superficial. We're more willing to listen to His voice, dig deeper into His Word, and entrust our lives to His faithfulness. Then the real adventure begins!

What is standing in the way of your moving forward in your Christian walk? Commit those things to He who is able to handle your concerns.

JUNE 12

Acknowledging our dependence on God is critical to godly living. That's what prayer is, you know—our declaration of dependence on God. Prayer says, "We need you Lord . . . *desperately.*"

Philippians 4:6 is a marvelous exhortation to pray in times of anxiety. Read it, and then pray it.

JUNE 13

During sweet times of fellowship with God, it's easy to think that we will always remember our thoughts and insights. But it isn't long before those certainties become submerged under a load of responsibilities. Don't lose sight of what you learn—those experiences make you deeper.

Today is a good day to commit your thoughts to God in a letter. Write of your love for Him, of your thanks to Him, and of your concerns.

June 14

These hot days of summer can turn into real scorchers if you don't seek out a restful change of pace. Take a break from the routine. You'll be the better for it—you'll think more clearly, sleep more soundly, and be primed for a season of real growth.

Fix yourself a cool drink with lots of ice. Then, allow the refreshment of Matthew 11:28 to wash over you.

June 15

Because He is acquainted with sorrow, the Savior is touched by your pain and weakness. His warnings, promises, and reminders give you hope when they are diligently applied.

Journal about God's faithfulness in times of darkness to gain encouragement for the future. Write about His work in your life.

June 16

God made fathers for a number of reasons. They are models of masculinity in a world that is fast losing touch with genuine manhood. They stand firm on principles of integrity in a society that has lost its character. They serve God faithfully. Who can possibly measure the influence of fathers who display character like that?

Deuteronomy 5:16 commands, "Honor your father." Ask God to help you honor your father in your actions and your heart.

June 17

Today our country pauses to say thanks to fathers. In spite of all the imperfections and inconsistencies apparent in the ranks, hats off to those who still try their best to be what they ought. The fathers whose children still need them, admire them, and love them dearly deserve their due praise.

Pray for the fathers you know, that they would be men of integrity, honor, and purity, and that they would love God and walk with Him.

June 18

Circumstances, needs, finances, relationships—all of these work together for God's glory when they're given to Him in prayer.

Grab a stack of 3x5 cards, and jot a prayer request on each. Tuck them into a purse, a wallet, a car visor, or your Bible in order to turn free moments into short prayer sessions.

June 19

There's something about remembering the past that strengthens our spirits for today and the future. The Bible is packed full of specific commands to remember— remember His faithfulness, His provision, His wonders, His sacrifice, His character. May frequent reminders of God's grace and love strengthen you for the days ahead.

Read Psalm 92:1-2, and practice it today.

June 20

Once we accept Christ as our substitute, our advocate, and our pathway to God, His death and resurrection become intensely personal. Like Paul, we make it our goal "to know [Christ] and the power of His resurrection and the fellowship of His sufferings, being conformed to His death" (Philippians 3:10).

It is difficult to meditate on the Cross, but few things are as profoundly moving. Take time to think about Christ's sacrifice today.

June 21

Just because God is unseen does not mean that He is disinterested or absent. Though absent physically, He is present in every believer, every movement, and every event. He faithfully proves Himself the Lord of His people.

Read and rejoice over Psalm 93.

June 22

Are you up for a personal challenge? When it comes to
charting the future, measure your success with these
questions: Lord, am I following Your directives? Am I
being sensitive to your guidance? Is my progress based
on Your purpose for my life? Are my fears overshadowed
by Your faithfulness?

*Open your calendar and apply the questions above to
your entries for the week. Are there adjustments
that need to be made?*

June 23

Few things in this life invite us to go deep. And yet, if
there's anything that we cannot afford in our walk with
God, it's shallowness. How wonderful it is to read God's
Word and find invitations to know Him more intimately,
to discover Him at work in our lives, to enter into His
presence.

*Meditate on 2 Timothy 2:16-17, and put it into action
in your life.*

JUNE 24

God certainly does work in mysterious ways in our lives. Sometimes it's an unexpected joy that emerges from great sorrow, or the unfolding of events that clear the way to a long-sought-after dream. If we were to sit down and swap stories about God's mysterious ways, I'm sure we would marvel at His sovereignty and goodness.

Look for an opportunity today to tell someone about God's past faithfulness in your life. Rejoice anew!

JUNE 25

The most famous and the most inconspicuous heroes of the Bible were people just like you and me who chose to be God's disciples. They were willing to learn from, follow, and imitate Him. More than anything, I pray that you are continuing to learn and grow in the truth to become more and more like Christ.

Have you withheld an area of your life from the Lord? Pray that He will help you relinquish ownership of that area to Him.

June 26

Two things never change: people's needs and the Bible's answers. The more things change, the more we need to focus on the eternal, unchanging solutions of trusting and obeying God.

Are you keeping on track with your daily Bible reading? Purpose again to be faithful with it.

June 27

Isn't it powerful to know God's faithfulness is "new every morning," just as the prophet Jeremiah wrote in Lamentations 3:23? It keeps coming up with the dawn, shining right in our faces.

The next phrase of Lamentations 3:23 reads, "Great is Your faithfulness." Wouldn't that be a great song to sing at the beginning of your day?

June 28

When the months turn hot and sticky, the refreshing breeze brings relief like nothing else. The heat is most fierce when we face exhausting days alone. Though Paul experienced scorching, lonely days during his ministry, his friends extended a cup of cool water in Jesus' name.

You don't need special strategies to reach the world for Christ; you simply need to love people the way Jesus loved them. Offer them the cool water of encouragement.

June 29

As we wait for eternity to unfold, let's encourage each other toward godliness. Then, as we stand before our Lord, we'll be able to hear Him say, "Well done, good and faithful servant."

Think of someone you know who has been a "good and faithful servant." Write that person a note of thanks and encouragement today.

June 30

Grace is a common word in the Christian vocabulary. We talk about it, sing about it, read and even preach about it. But the best way to communicate grace is through our actions.

Are you full of grace? Are you known as a gracious person? Purpose grace in your speech and in your actions today.

July 1

We can learn a lot about living life from Paul's example. Paul was neither grim in his countenance nor frightened about his future. Stretched across his "yes" face was a joyful smile of contentment. The man didn't merely endure life . . . he *enjoyed* it.

Look in the mirror more than once today. Do you find yourself wearing your "yes" face?

July 2

When you don't win . . . when you find yourself unable to bounce back . . . when it seems as though you will never make it through, God becomes real, and His grace proves sufficient.

Are you feeling defeated? Share your struggles with another and allow God's grace to comfort you through their godly counsel.

July 3

My heart skips a beat when I realize that someone, somewhere, maybe at this very moment, is hearing of Jesus Christ for the first time in his or her life. What a magnificent thought!

The church began to grow in Acts 2:37-47. Why was the apostles' ministry so effective? How can you apply this to your ministry opportunities?

July 4

A nation is only as strong as her homes. And, as Paul warned in 2 Timothy 3:1, "difficult times will come" in these last days. Scripture warns us of this so that we will deal responsibly and even courageously with wrong, whenever and wherever it surfaces.

Has an area of compromise entered your home? Take measures today to correct it.

July 5

Hope is necessary to life. Without it, we shrivel up and die. Hope is what we need when we face seasons of illness, financial hardship, disappointments, unemployment, or the loss of someone close to us.

God's grace and the fellowship of His hope are evident for you in the words of I Peter I:3-5.

July 6

Most of the Christian life is not big-time tingles. It's not cheers and applause from the crowd. It's not relaxed, easy living. It means gutting it out, hanging tough, trusting God to work in and through our lives in spite of the times in which we live. Let me assure you—He will. He places a high priority on endurance.

God will give you the strength to endure if you trust in Him. Offer Him the concerns of your heart and ask for added endurance.

July 7

The Lord uses you to help accomplish His work throughout the earth. The sweet smell of the Lord is spread abroad, but traces of the aroma linger with you. May the fragrance of God's grace permeate your life today and linger on all that you touch.

*Where does God's sweet aroma linger in your life?
Where does it need to be introduced?
Carry His grace with you.*

JULY 8

View life from the position of joyful winsomeness. That doesn't mean you won't live in the real world. Hardly! But it does mean that you will reflect the reality of a life set free from sin and its doom.

Who needs to hear about the freedom that is found in Christ? Offer them this hope today.

JULY 9

For most of my adult life, I've kept a record of the conversations I've had with my Father. The practice of keeping this journal facilitates God's peace in my life. Consider writing down your prayers to God—that way, you'll never lose track of the best things you learn from Him.

Write out a prayer. Share your hopes, your hurts, your trials, and your victories with your heavenly Father.

July 10

Is your passion for God waning? Pay attention to the things that matter. Address the real needs in your life. Come to terms with wrong, wherever you may have tolerated it. Ask God to bring cleansing, purity, wholeness, and a full restoration of your walk with Him.

Meditate on Psalm 40.

July 11

A pursuit can be so intense that it dominates one's life. We are working hand in hand with our Lord each day as we address issues, provoke thoughts, challenge others toward holy living, and shine a bright light of hope to all who live in spiritual darkness.

Raise the bar for holy living in your life. As you do, challenge those around you to increase their faithfulness as well.

July 12

God is forever on a quest to conform us "to the image of His Son" (Romans 8:29) — to see His character traits developed in our lives. And the One who began this pursuit isn't about to abandon it. We are His workmanship, and He is intensely committed to us!

Do you know what God is cultivating in you?
Read Galatians 5:22-23.

July 13

God desires that those who love Him also live by His moral precepts. More and more Christians are setting aside their standards of moral excellence for the hollow promises of an immoral lifestyle — but God's standards have not changed. He continues to be a God of holiness.

Has it been tough for you to keep those standards strong?
Ask God for forgiveness right now.
Seek to live in purity.

July 14

There is a whole world of people who need the hope that we have in order to survive. Become compelled to reach . . . to touch . . . and perhaps even to share with them that which turns mere existence into meaningful living.

Look for opportunities to put your faith into action today so that it offers a tangible hope to others.

July 15

Determine that certain things will not change. Maintain a complete reliance on the Lord rather than on the arm of the flesh, a faithful adherence to the Word of God rather than human opinion, and an uncompromising life of integrity rather than deceit or hypocrisy. Make these things your non-negotiables.

Dependence on the Lord . . . adherence to the Word of God . . . a life of integrity. How can you model these actions more in your life today?

July 16

During some seasons of the year, when harvest is a long way off and not much growth is seen on the vine, abiding can seem tiring and tedious. But the faithful farmer sticks with it month after month, season after season.

Continue to grow and abide in Christ.
Read John 15:1-11.

July 17

In a day like ours—when shallow thinking, superficial faith, and secret-service saints litter the landscape—it is imperative that we keep ourselves from passive indifference. The watchword for today? **Be on the alert!** We must be people of deep conviction, regardless of the cost or the consequences.

Have you found yourself yielding to complacency
in your faith? Combat that temptation with the
wellspring of God's Word.

JULY 18

A number of people in Scripture were nourished by another's contribution. Elijah recovered from his brief lapse in faith, thanks to Elisha's contribution of companionship. David gained encouragement from Jonathan's contribution of time and friendship. By sharing our treasures, we add strength and support to one another on the journey.

Who are you nourishing in your life? Reach out.
Share your life with another.

JULY 19

When Christ returns for the church, He will bring together the resurrected believers and those who have not experienced physical death. Whether we pass away before the Rapture or live until His return, we will soon be with Him. Either way, what a blessed hope we have!

Do you wonder what you will behold in heaven?
Read about it in Revelation 21:1-4.

July 20

I often return to those familiar first pages of Scripture. God was creating, working, and sovereignly moving from one day to the next. His creative touch included scenes of breathtaking beauty. I never cease to marvel at those miraculous events in which all things began directly from His hands.

Enjoy the sunrise or sunset today. Look closely at the leaves that hang on the trees. Enjoy the work of His hands.

July 21

David had his friend Jonathan. Jesus had His disciples. Paul had Luke, Silas, and Timothy. These friends helped make life bearable for those with whom they worked because they shouldered some of the load. We cannot make it without our partners in the journey.

Have you allowed another to shoulder with you on the journey? Find a friend that will challenge you, strengthen you, and pray for you.

July 22

From the first century to the fifteenth, the Word of God was passed by word of mouth or written on parchment. Within the last five hundred years, it has become accessible to millions. In all things, the message has remained the same: Receive grace through faith in Christ.

Want to strengthen your confidence in Scripture?
Read 2 Timothy 3:16-17.

July 23

Few things are more effective at diffusing the tyranny of expectations than the realization that we are loved. As people discover how much God loves them, their own sense of self-worth increases . . . which frees them to give love to others. It becomes a contagious chain reaction.

Who in your life needs to feel loved? By accepting them
as they are, they will find a safe
haven in your presence.

July 24

"God loves a cheerful giver" (2 Corinthians 9:7).
Literally, the phrase reads "for the hilarious giver God
prizes." For far too long, God's people have been shamed
and whipped into giving. People give . . . but not hilar-
iously. God highly prizes those who give with "joy, joy,
joy, joy down in their hearts."

Tithing offers an opportunity to grow your faith.
Trust God with your finances, and give generously today.

July 25

How often Scripture urges us to grow up! As we grow
up, we learn to think of others, to share in the workload,
to be thoughtful, to stay calm during stressful times. My
prayer for you is that spiritual depth might become the
distinguishing mark of your growth toward maturity.

How are you growing up? Does your faith characterize
your lifestyle? Identify a key area where your faith
needs to be more evident.

July 26

God is the One who imprints His will on our lives—and on the world. As Paul wrote to the Ephesians, it is God who "made known to us the mystery of His will, according to His kind intention" (Ephesians 1:9).

God's fingerprints are all around us . . . in the clouds, the rivers, and every living being. Give thanks to Him for His marvelous work.

July 27

The greatest hope we have is the certainty that one day we will be with Him. This hope is fact—you can anticipate it as you did this morning's sunrise.

What do you anticipate about your future in heaven? Tell your Father all your thoughts concerning that day.

July 28

Wherever we turn in the Bible, the remembering theme repeats itself—remember God's faithfulness, His provision, His wonders, His sacrifice, His character. When we deliberately remember these significant truths, the challenges that await us today and tomorrow fall into perspective with God's character.

Reflect on His faithfulness throughout the ages as you read Isaiah 63:7-14.

July 29

The joyful Christian who thinks straight and stays clean is a model of Christ to the world. It is through you that the world sees God.

What can you do to show Christ's love, grace, acceptance, patience, or compassion to someone today?

July 30

God chooses to minister to people's needs through the gifting, servanthood, and generosity of the body of Christ. Through you, His Word reflects a light that few know in this world shrouded in gray.

Have you discovered your spiritual gift?
Find your unique gifting in I Corinthians 12:4-11.

July 31

Whatever God is doing in your heart comes from your willingness to embrace His truth. I want to encourage you today to let Him do His work. Welcome it, even when it's tough. You'll be so glad you did.

What work is God doing in your heart?
Are you accepting it? Allow His intentions for your
growth to take root in your life.

August 1

The Bible is loaded with events and examples of people whom God appointed and anointed to fill roles of leadership—and He still desires to use special men and women to do His work! He is forever on the lookout for those who are godly, courageous, and willing to lead.

Pray for your pastor and the leaders of your church today.

August 2

My hope is that you, as a soldier and servant of Christ, will not shrink in fear as you represent Him. And my prayer is that you will be encouraged, though foes abound in this vile world. May His grace sustain you.

Read Ephesians 2:10, and be encouraged by it!

August 3

What does it mean to really live? It means that we become joyful in gratitude, earnest in prayer, abounding in love, and established in holiness (1 Thessalonians 3:8–13). Nothing else surpasses these goals—especially since we *really* live if we put them into practice.

I Thessalonians 3:8 calls us to "stand firm in the Lord." In what ways will you stand firm in the coming week?

August 4

Relationships were designed by God to be gardens of fragrant flowers that blossom into harmony, beauty, and unity. How are your relationships growing? Cultivate them well, and give them sufficient time and attention so that they blossom with a sweet aroma.

Write a note of encouragement to a friend today, letting them know they are in your prayers. And don't forget to pray for their needs and spiritual growth.

August 5

When you rest in the Lord, relief from the searing rays of adversity is found under His sheltering shade. And what begins as an attitude easily becomes a ministry, bringing much-needed relief and refreshment to another's heated, stressful day.

Psalm 91 speaks of dwelling in the shelter of the Most High. Crawl into the shade of the Lord, and be refreshed by these verses.

August 6

The major battle of the Christian life is balancing our kingdom vision with all the things that make us anxious and occupy too much of our time and attention. And that is precisely why Jesus warned, "No one can serve two masters" (Matthew 6:24).

In what ways do you find yourself serving two masters? Bring this concern before the Lord and listen to His counsel.

August 7

No question about it, affirmation spurs us on. It deepens our determination. It confirms our worth and personal significance. God made us like that. Knowing us to be creatures who long for affirmation, He filled His Book with words of encouragement.

There is someone who needs your encouragement today. Don't put off writing that note or making that phone call to brighten their day.

August 8

Your personal intercession for the needs of others changes things. As you pray, God ignites the truth of His Word and brings power—life-changing power—to the lives of those in need.

A prayer journal is a wonderful place to record God's work. Write down your requests, and make a note of it as they are answered. Watch your faith grow!

August 9

Know that He will be faithful to strengthen you in your walk and prosper you in your way when you commit your heart and your deeds to Him alone.

Meditate on Philippians 2:13:
"For it is God who is at work in you, both to will and to work for His good pleasure."

August 10

Realizing that we occasionally run full speed in the wrong direction, God forgives us as we come to Him in our need. Knowing we are weak, He promises us strength. He promises that future rewards will be ours to claim when we stand in His presence. Again and again, He assures us of His unconditional love.

Have you realized how much God delights in you?
He is eager for relationship, quick to forgive, unfailing in His love. Let that thought encourage you.

August 11

Growing tall, growing up, growing broad—what great signs of health! But for the Christian, depth is the prerequisite for stability and strength. Grow deep in your walk. Grow deep in your commitment. Grow deep in your knowledge of and love for the Lord Jesus Christ and His will for your life.

Growing deep — and going deep — in the Christian life takes time. Can you block out a specific time each day to spend alone with God?

August 12

There's something about remembering the past that strengthens our spirits today. I pray that frequent reminders of His grace and love will strengthen you for the days ahead.

Think about the person who first shared the Good News with you. Pray for them today.

August 13

Our adversary is clever and brilliant, and he is relentless—even ruthless—in using every means possible to get us off target. But I want to assure you that the power and grace of the almighty God can strengthen you against Satan's schemes. As you commit, so you will remain.

Read about the armor of God in Ephesians 6:10-17 as you prepare to face the world today.

August 14

Threatening, stormy times like ours resemble an angry and restless ocean. As never before, we need a bright, sure lighthouse . . . a trustworthy signal offering safety, purpose, and meaning. If the ship of humanity has ever searched for a harbor of hope, today is the day.

Here's an amazing thought from Matthew 5:14: "You are the light of the world. A city set on a hill cannot be hidden." Let's live like it!

August 15

There is nothing quite like studying the life of Jesus, is there? Whether relaxed or in a pressurized situation, He never failed to demonstrate true character. Perhaps the only thing better than studying His life is emulating it.

Take a look at your daily life.
Would those around you recognize you as a Christian?
How can you be more Christlike today?

August 16

Although history and cultures vary, our needs are the same: We need to know God and His Word.

Psalm 119 is filled with reasons to dig into the
Word. Read it today, or over the next few days.

August 17

We need something tangible to bring us back to the green pastures and quiet waters that restore our souls. As Psalm 23 reminds us, it is during the quiet times that we remember anew that the Lord is our Shepherd and that He is in command of our lives.

Read Psalm 23, line by line, and thank the Lord for each promise found therein.

August 18

Children need models. They are like human sponges, ready to soak up whatever surrounds them. My hope is that you are gaining sufficient biblical truth and personal stimulation to help you become spiritually contagious, spreading the right germs to all within your sphere of influence—especially those under your roof.

The greatest gift a parent can give a child is their prayers. Approach the throne of heaven on behalf of your children.

August 19

There's a race to be conquered. According to 1 Corinthians 16:13, we must "be on the alert" against our aggressive adversary, "stand firm" because nothing is conquered without commitment, "act like men" because childishness won't cut it in battle, and "be strong" because weakness and surrender are only inches apart . . . and quitting isn't an option.

In what way should you be on the alert today? Commit this to prayer, and stand firm in doing what is right.

August 20

Do you have any idea how many of your fellow Christians are thinking of falling away from the living God? No, I don't either. But we can be used of God to keep their hearts from hardening as we encourage them day after day and week after week. God promises that!

Read 1 Peter 1:14-16.
Count the number of times the word "holy" is used.

August 21

When we depend on each other, we have a good return for our labor, we lift one another up, we keep each other warm, and we are better able to resist an attack (Ecclesiastes 4:9–12). In companionship we find mutual effort, mutual support, mutual comfort, and mutual strength.

Have you ever made a list of the "one anothers" found in the New Testament? Start listing them: love one another, encourage one another, care for one another . . .

August 22

Virtually everywhere we turn, we find the twin demons of a too-busy society—isolationism and loneliness—that bring about a decline in companionship and interest in others. In our isolated, lonely world, most everyone would benefit from relationship investments that yield satisfying dividends.

Fellowshipping with other Christians for refreshment, growth, and accountability is important. Now might be a good time to join a Bible study or small group.

AUGUST 23

When you make a consistent study of the Scriptures, your relationship with God becomes intimate, deep, and wonderfully satisfying. By His grace, your growth will continue. And this growth is available to all who dare to be different, who are willing to pay the price in time and effort.

Find someone willing to partner with you as you read the Scriptures. Accountability is a valuable investment for all those involved.

AUGUST 24

The summer season offers great opportunities to deepen our walks with God. Take a solo jaunt around the block in fellowship with the Lord. Light up that barbecue with a passion to share Christ with your neighbors. And by all means, stay in the Word. It's the only surefire way to keep these days from blowing you dry.

Read Psalm I. Choose a verse — or the entire Psalm — to memorize. It will keep your leaves from withering!

August 25

Consider the story of Esther. One woman—one voice—saved the life of her nation. Her answer? "I will go . . . and if I perish, I perish" (Esther 4:16). As is true of every person who stands in the gap, she was willing to be personally involved, even to the point of great sacrifice.

Perhaps God is calling you to be the person He will use in this place and time. Ask Him, and listen for His response.

August 26

Nothing is happening on earth that brings a surprise to heaven. Nothing touches us that has not first passed through the fingers of His hands. Things that seem altogether confusing, without reason, unfair, or even wrong do indeed fit into the Father's providential plan.

The Phillips translation of James 1:2 exhorts us to "welcome [trials] as friends." That's hard to do, isn't it? Hard . . . but not impossible.

AUGUST 27

Just as cleanliness is next to godliness, simplicity is next to integrity. The longer I live, the more I appreciate the simple things in life . . . and the more I admire those who keep things simple.

Breathe deeply. Enjoy the sunset. And invite someone you love to share those moments with you.

AUGUST 28

Are you satisfied with your Christian walk? Think before you answer. Take time to look below the surface of all the things you are doing and ponder who you are becoming. Are you genuinely pleased with what you see? Be painfully honest with yourself.

If you were a doctor, you might write yourself a prescription for improving your spiritual health. What would the prescription include?

AUGUST 29

Just as faith without works is dead, so words without concern and compassion are empty. Let's cater words of encouragement to those who are hungry for tangible expressions of love—the intimate and affectionate expressions of our hearts.

In every possible situation, see how often you can speak words of encouragement today.

AUGUST 30

One trait characterizes Jesus more than any other: *authentic servanthood*. Rather than making a name for Himself, defending His right, or promoting His cause, the Savior served others. May I encourage you today to be a servant? There is no better way to represent a pace-setting model of unselfishness in a world of self-serving mediocrity.

Watch for opportunities to be of service today. And thank God for providing those chances.

August 31

Abiding enables us to be fruitful for the Lord. His qualities become expressed through our lives. Serving one another, giving to one another, helping, supporting, and encouraging one another . . . these things form the outflow—the fruit—of a heart that abides faithfully in the Lord.

Read Hebrews 10:24-25, and "consider" its practical counsel.

September 1

Ours is a day of impersonal crowds. Our identity is more often connected to where we went to school and what we do for a living than to who we really are. How different it is in God's forever family! Let's never forget that that is where we find our ultimate purpose and unconditional acceptance.

You will always be accepted in God's family.
Read Romans 8:14-17 for reassurance.

September 2

Most of us are more familiar with domestic weakness than with the characteristics of a strong home. It's true, however, that strong families spend time together, communicate well, express appreciation, have a spiritual commitment, and are able to solve problems in a crisis. Take a look at that list. Think about your family.

What brings strength to your family?
Identify an area of weakness, and consider how you might work to strengthen it.

September 3

Who hasn't swallowed that lump in the throat when reading about the return of the Prodigal Son? After such a long wait and without announcement, there he stood. Stooped. Dirty. Needy. Ashamed. But eyes that once burned in anger were soothed in tears as relief on both sides erased all fear.

Though difficult, accepting someone who ran away provides an outlet for God's grace to shine through you. Who needs your embrace today?

SEPTEMBER 4

We cannot abide this life without each other. The encouragement of the body of Christ fuels our fire and reminds us that we are not alone.

Want to know the secret to a thriving ministry? Keep communication fluid, misunderstandings minimal, and enthusiasm set to maximum. Let your commitment outshine any conflicts.

SEPTEMBER 5

As new and fresh as this season may be, some things simply continue on. Not subject to seasonal changes, our mandate is to "be ready in season and out of season" (2 Timothy 4:2).

Are you ready to share your faith when the occasion arises? Write down the things that give you confidence in God.

SEPTEMBER 6

Many times we don't understand why God didn't step in or why He did so in such an unusual manner. It often takes hindsight to understand His answers and appreciate His faithfulness.

Do you know someone who is having difficulty understanding God's ways? Be a listening ear for them while they seek to understand His intentions.

SEPTEMBER 7

Aren't you grateful that the Lord has called you—called you by name—into His kingdom? How natural, then, to thank Him for revealing His Word to you, for spreading His love throughout the world so that you could hear His message and surrender your heart in gratitude to Him!

Reflect upon the events that led to your salvation. Thank Him for providing the way to His heart.

September 8

When we're abiding, we're living each moment connected to and in relationship with the Lord Himself. Nothing illustrates our complete dependence on Him more than this word.

Make it the natural beat of your heart to connect each moment, each thought, and each interaction with others to your relationship with the Lord.

September 9

Even though we began the year intending to slow down and guard against a calendar of too many activities, we still find ourselves involved in the rat race. This autumn may find us on a treadmill of daily deadlines that is, at times, spinning out of control.

Identify where you first overcommitted your schedule. What might you reduce in order to provide yourself with a more balanced, healthy lifestyle?

September 10

I would most like to see changes occur within the homes of people all around this aching world . . . changes in relationships between husbands and wives, in commitments to family values, in attitudes toward children, and in respect for parents.

How is your family shining the light of Christ?
May it model Philippians 2:14-16.

September 11

Remarkable changes occur in a life once the liberating power of Christ takes hold. Liberty—Christ's promise of our being set free—is worth fighting for, so it is worth whatever it takes to make it known. Grace killers need to be exposed!

Are you stomping out the relief God's grace can bring
to a hurting heart? Correct your actions, and be
an example of His love for them.

September 12

I'm convinced that a "grace awakening" can set the message of Christ ablaze more than any other means imaginable. Think of the joy that would emerge and the contagious charm that would free people of the legalism that kills the message of grace.

Ask God for an awakening of grace that might sweep its way around the world. Open yourself up to becoming His instrument to those around you.

September 13

Live the Word. Whether it's spring or autumn, convenient or not. Whether you've got a cheering section or you're alone. Stay true to the life to which Christ has called you and model the Word in your daily attitudes and responses.

Though you may feel alone when modeling the life of Christ, you are joined with the worldwide body of Christ, as Paul said in I Corinthians 1:3-7.

September 14

Nothing is needed more in our world than clear evidence of God's love. In fact, you and I are where people first look for it. They watch our lives, listen to our words, and examine our motives, whether we realize it or not. They're looking for love in action.

How can you demonstrate love in action today? Offer a kind word, a gentle response, a selfless action, a patient attitude.

September 15

When God moves in, He moves in unannounced. He bursts upon the soul, bringing forgiveness, cleansing, peace, and a whole new perspective and dimension. He calls it "eternal life."

How has your perspective changed since you've known Christ? Write these things down—they are the evidence of your growth.

September 16

Two things give me great joy: the promise that God's Word will never return void and the knowledge that God uses us to accomplish His will. You and I are blessed to play a part in His amazing plan, aren't we?

You are an important part of God's plan for the world. What part is He asking you to play in your corner of the neighborhood?

September 17

Reflection and evaluation represent hard work. It's much easier to increase speed, press forward, and take on more assignments. But I have found that the Lord honors our times of quietness.

Pause and reflect on your life. Are you growing, or are you moving too quickly to see His work and hear His words? Quiet your spirit before Him.

SEPTEMBER 18

It's those evidences of God's grace that take the edge off the stressful realities of life. Can you help but smile when you realize that someone you'll meet someday in heaven had his or her destiny changed when they responded to God's Word?

Begin to view those around you as lost souls that need salvation. When your love reaches out, they may find eternity within an arm's length.

SEPTEMBER 19

Willful bondage—long-standing habits of stubborn and unbending attitudes—are secretly cultivated in homes lacking harmony and happiness. But Christ came to break the bondage that has ensnared their lives. It doesn't happen quickly or easily, but the Savior does set them free, exactly as He promised.

You partner with God in His work when you pray for those who have unyielding hearts. Pray for God to release the enslaving bonds that shackle them.

SEPTEMBER 20

In God's family, every one of us is considered gifted.
Regardless of social status, age, personality, or resources,
you are gifted. Every believer has been given a manifesta-
tion of the Spirit.

*Use your spiritual gift. Whether through teaching,
encouraging, giving, or praying, your gift is needed
for the work of the Spirit.*

SEPTEMBER 21

Whenever I have asked others to share a time when they
grew spiritually and emotionally, they always mention the
tough times. We don't often name great victories as
teachers of great benefits. Pain is a tough but faithful
teacher.

*Think back on a difficult time in your life. Though
painful, what did you learn from it? How was it
used by God for your growth?*

SEPTEMBER 22

We live in a day when the majority of hungry souls are given empty promises and sold a bill of goods. Lots of trinkets and gimmicks, but no solid substance to sustain life. The result is tragic. When difficulties arise, they lack the spiritual strength to cope. It takes nourishing food to survive.

Offer a hungry soul food that truly nourishes — the Bread of Life. Share Christ with another, and follow up on their growth continuously.

SEPTEMBER 23

Making the family a priority involves sacrifice. It takes sweat and determination for married couples to stay together, for parents to invest time in their children's lives, and for single parents to endure tough days and lonely evenings. Thankfully, God's Word is relevant for your needs—it will help you laugh at life rather than dread it.

God's Word gives you the assurance you need to get through tough times. Let the words of I Peter 1:6-9 encourage you this day.

SEPTEMBER 24

The Master is neither mute nor careless as He alters our times and changes our seasons. He often speaks in a still, small voice and, through various sections of His Word, makes known His will and His ways.

Do you know how to hear God's voice? Quiet your heart as you sit before Him, and allow the truths of His Word to fill you.

SEPTEMBER 25

What is a spiritual gift? It's an ability from God that allows you to carry out a particular function in the family of God with ease and effectiveness.

In what ways has God gifted you? Reflect on the things that come naturally to you. How might you use that gift in ministry?

September 26

May our Lord give you three blessings this fall: a time of refreshment with your family, a renewed sense of delight in your work, and a deep and abiding peace before your God. My hope is that these blessings will help you keep at it, day in and day out.

Refreshment, renewal, and peace come through the time you carve out to gain sustenance from the Father.
Read Psalm 65:9-13.

September 27

God teaches us His Word in the context of our own world. In other words, He is as personal as our individual needs.

What are the needs of those closest to you?
Search the Scriptures for sweet words of wisdom to offer them.

September 28

Through storm or through calm, God will faithfully provide for our needs. He will calm our storms. He will take care of our families. He will provide what's necessary. And in return, He asks for our trust.

Do you believe that He will do these things for you? Let the words of Ezekiel 34:11-16 establish a heart of trust in you.

September 29

Let's invite Jesus' love into each step we take. I like how J. B. Phillips paraphrases it: "The very spring of our actions is the love of Christ" (2 Corinthians 5:14).

What motivates you to act — Christ's love or your glory? Keep His love at the forefront of your mind, that it may be reflected in your actions.

September 30

Whether the Gospel is heard for the first time or the hundredth, people hunger and thirst for it. The reason? Because of its core message of life, of people, of joy, of love.

What is it about the gospel message that captivates you? Share that with another today.

October 1

We're not strong horses ready for combat or sneaky panthers that pounce on our prey. We're just sheep— clumsy, awkward, and not all that bright! But we have the perfect Shepherd who is good, faithful, and even great.

Read John 10:14-15. Thank Jesus for being your Shepherd.

October 2

Did you know that the word *grace* means *gift*? Literally, it is by God's gift that you have been saved (Ephesians 2:8). It's no wonder that we give so naturally once we get a grasp on grace—and in turn, God gives back to us again. He doesn't match gift for gift, but goes beyond it in an abundance of ways.

One of the fullest measures of grace is given when you forgive after being wounded or wronged. Let the Holy Spirit help you extend grace through forgiveness.

October 3

Tough times bring out the best in all of us. When you persevere in trials, God develops your trust and obedience—models of determination emerge when the going gets tough. Lean on Him through hard times.

As you read James 1:2-4, note what the "testing of your faith" produces.

October 4

View every gift from God as a direct result of His faithful provision for your needs. Once we accept the foundational fact that God owns it all, it is amazing how quickly our priorities fall into place.

Read James 1:17.
Underline the word "every."

October 5

Do you need to recover your pioneer spirit? Do you need to break free from some long-standing area of spiritual timidity or a disobedient lifestyle and cut a new trail—a pioneer trail—for God's glory? Become a pioneer of faith, courage, and independence in your day-to-day walk with Christ among your peers today.

Today is a good day to take a risk — invite the
participation of the Holy Spirit,
and get ready for an adventure!

October 6

It was Solomon who wrote, "He who walks in integrity walks securely, But he who perverts his ways will be found out" (Proverbs 10:9). Deep down in our souls, what we look for and what we long for is *character*. When it is lacking, we feel it. It is the "given" in greatness.

Make a point of communicating appreciation to someone in your life who has exemplified godly character.

October 7

Don't give up, and don't be anxious. Why? Because He is faithful. Keep on encouraging one another to love and good deeds. How often? More and more as the days go by.

Make the most of your time today — model the truth of Ephesians 5:15-21.

October 8

What is your favorite feeling? Mine is the feeling of accomplishment. Is there anything better than thinking, "I'm through—mission accomplished"? It's what Jesus must have felt when He prayed, "I glorified You on the earth, having accomplished the work which You have given Me to do" (John 17:4).

Think back to the accomplishments in which you take the most pride. Think ahead to the goals you still have. Talk to God about both.

October 9

We are His sheep. When we hear His voice, we follow His leading and trust in Him instead of leaning on our own understanding. He watches over us because we're in His flock: "We are His people and the sheep of His pasture" (Psalm 100:3).

Memorize Psalm 100 this week. It is only six verses, but it's full of praise to the Lord.

OCTOBER 10

I'm intrigued by those first-century disciples of Jesus.
Their willingness to drop everything and follow Him is
nothing short of remarkable. What was it about Jesus that
created such magnetic appeal? It was Himself. It was who
He was, what He modeled, and how He conducted
Himself—He was so very different from all the rest!

How did God first call you to follow Him?
Praise Him for pursuing you.

OCTOBER 11

Remember the last time you gave someone that perfect
gift? I bet sheer delight was written all over your face. And
of course, watching the other person's face break out in a
grin of surprise, revealing a special surge of gratitude—
well, I'd call that grace in action.

Grace is the extension of unmerited favor.
Watch for an opportunity to give grace to another today.

OCTOBER 12

God specializes in the unfathomable, and He is full of surprises! He works day after day and year after year to bring about His purpose. Frankly, I'm excited about what He will do in the future—and I wouldn't be as excited as I am if I could explain His ways!

Read Isaiah 55:8-9.
What valuable words to memorize!

OCTOBER 13

You can be sure that God is deepening and strengthening you for the days ahead. He is sovereignly and compassionately at work, getting you ready for His purposes yet to be revealed.

Have you ever prayed through your calendar?
Open its pages and pray over each event
of the coming week.

October 14

When we're caught up in our daily responsibilities, it's easy to forget that those around us need eternal life—and that they need to be told where to find it. That's just what you're doing when you share God's Word to a dying world.

Matthew 28:18-20 contains what we term the Great Commission. How can you be a "Great Commission Christian" today?

October 15

Each time it's told, the story of Christ's love is more wonderfully sweet. Why? Because none of us ever tire of hearing that we are loved. Not one of us fathoms the depths of God's love.

Maybe there is someone in your circle who needs to hear that you love them. Remind them of God's love for them as well.

October 16

Autumn's warmth, color, and crispness seem to indicate the Lord's nudging us to get ready for midwinter's blast —visible or invisible. Being so warned, we can prepare ourselves ahead of time. Wise are the ones who do so!

The book of Proverbs is full of good advice.
Consider Proverbs 6:6-11 and the life lesson
that comes through watching the ant prepare for winter.

October 17

Quietness and solitude help renew our perspective when we get bogged down. I have discovered that a few long walks, a good book, and time spent under the open sky refresh my spirit like nothing else. Our Lord planned it that way. He knew that the therapy of His handiwork would soothe our souls if we would take the time to enjoy it.

Make it a priority this week to spend
a few minutes enjoying God's creation.
Breathe deeply. Love gratefully.

October 18

There comes a point when you realize that the words of that treasured hymn fit your life right here, right now: "'Tis grace hath brought me safe thus far, and grace will lead me home." The grace that has brought you "safe thus far" is still your guardian and guide. Grip grace tightly as you step into tomorrow and beyond.

Read John 14:16-17. Praise God for the indwelling presence of the Holy Spirit, who daily interprets grace in your life.

October 19

Is your life windy these days? The winds of change, adversity, and heightened demands and expectations can leave us feeling windblown. Take heart. As my mother used to say, "The roots grow deep when the winds are strong."

How is God deepening your roots? Specifically thank Him for that today.

October 20

Young children learn early that winning is the path to rewards and losing brings consequences too disappointing for words. Now that I'm older and have tasted a few victories and several defeats, I have to say that I've learned much more through losing than I have through winning.

It's not too late to thank God for the valleys through which you've already walked.
What looks differently in hindsight?

October 21

Since autumn has arrived, let me suggest that you take a few extra moments to reflect on the "giving trees" in your life. Thank God for faithful and encouraging sources of hope that stayed close during your growing-up years as a Christian. Then, after reflecting, consider giving in return.

Maybe your church needs Sunday school teachers or an open home for a neighborhood children's club. This might be the time for you to lead little children.

OCTOBER 22

Reflect back over the months that are now mere memories. Have there been any significant changes? How about growth? Maybe you've been forced to trust in the Lord in order to stop leaning on your own understanding. Hasn't God been good? Aren't you grateful that He has stayed by your side?

Memorize Proverbs 3:5-6.
Rejoice in those words!

OCTOBER 23

It is my passion that believers remain in touch with the issues of our times, bringing the Bible to bear not only upon the exposure of wrong, but also upon the hope that is found in Christ. By God's grace, we shall continue to make a difference in the cutting edge of our times.

If you are not consistently in prayer for our country and its leaders, now is a good time to begin.

October 24

Preserve a written record of divine interventions—times
when God taught and ministered to you in ways you
never dreamed He could. Why? So that the next time
you're walking straight into the wind, you'll remember
God's faithfulness and grow deeper.

*Scripture exhorts us to tell our children of God's
faithfulness. Share that with the children
in your life today!*

October 25

I've discovered that it doesn't take long for the new to get
old or even for something as fresh as autumn to grow
stale. We must renew our perspective on a consistent basis.

*Read Romans 12:1-2.
How can you renew your mind today?*

OCTOBER 26

It's not the number of activities that bothers us as much as the lack of satisfaction that accompanies them. As one of my mentors used to say, "Many of our activities are nothing more than a cheap anesthetic to deaden the pain of an empty life." Jesus said that He came to give us life . . . to the max!

If fasting is not one of your spiritual disciplines, consider fasting for just one meal. Use the time to read or pray.

OCTOBER 27

I've learned that a good sense of humor is essential to renew our perspective. When life is kept lighthearted by joy, everything else we encounter is remarkably impacted.

Cultivate your sense of humor. Look for all the ways God might delight you today with a laugh.

October 28

For all of you who are doing the right thing day in and day out, yet aren't receiving any praise—take heart! God's eternal rewards include a recognition of faithfulness . . . which is another way of saying, "First the cross, then the crown."

Read Revelation 8:1-6. The incense of the prayers of the saints is powerful. That is a wonderful way to worship today: in prayer.

October 29

If you are like me, getting lost in the shuffle of sameness sounds as exciting as ordering a plain vanilla cone at an ice cream store known for its thirty-one flavors. Who needs dull mediocrity if there's a chance at pace-setting rarity?

Find a believing friend, and make plans that are out-of-the-ordinary. Dare something big for our big God.

October 30

Evaluate your walk with God. If you sense that you're tolerating things you once resisted, establish yourself once again in holiness. Not until that slice of your life is in place will you "stand firm in the Lord" (1 Thessalonians 3:8). And only then can you expect to *really* live.

Take time to evaluate the ways in which you are growing as a believer. Is your life marked by holiness and righteousness or by complacency and ritual?

October 31

Have you ever noticed the important role children play in the Bible? Because He cares about them, so should we. Because He gives them such a high profile in His Book, so must we remember to include them when we make known the Gospel.

Today, pray for the children you know. Pray that faithful Christians will remain in their lives to love them and to guide them.

November 1

November is a good month to ask, "What are you thankful for?" Psalm 103 reminds us to be thankful that God forgives our sins, heals our diseases, redeems our lives, crowns us with love and compassion, satisfies us with good things, and works righteousness and justice. Wow—what a list!

Read through Psalm 103.
Make a list of the promises for which
you are most thankful.

November 2

When geese fly south for the winter, it's their natural instinct to work together. Whether rotating, flapping, helping, or honking, the flock is in it together—which enables them to accomplish what they set out to do. In the same way, we need each other. Our "flight pattern" works well only if all of us participate.

With whom are you flying these days?
How is your rotation and flight pattern glorifying God
and edifying all the members of the flock?

November 3

Someday, my friend, the story of God's love "will be our theme in glory—to tell the old, old story of Jesus and His love." Then, like now, we will stand together and proclaim His grace.

How is the story of God's love weaving its way through your life? Share it with someone today in preparation for what is ahead in glory.

November 4

Over and again, I am reminded of Paul's outrageous joy. Was it because he had it made? Hardly. Because he was free of suffering, disappointment, and difficulties? Not on your life. He wasn't living under his circumstances, but above them. His focus on Christ was strong and sure.

Take your cue from Paul's example by applying the words of 2 Corinthians 12:7-10 to your life.

November 5

For families to stay close, relate freely, and enjoy each other, they must unselfishly enter into one another's world and leave room for just plain fun—and they must take time to feel each other's pain. As the old Swedish motto puts it, "Shared joy is a double joy; shared sorrow is half a sorrow."

Are the squabbles in your family surpassing the joy you find in each other's company? Take the first step — model a great attitude.

November 6

Isn't God awesome? Only He could have linked our lives so intimately as Christian brothers and sisters through our love for Him. His perfect plan for you is a plan that no one else could have orchestrated. A God that loving and holy deserves nothing less than all we have to give.

What do you need to release to God's control today? Release it to Him as you remember that He diligently cares for the events of your life.

November 7

Whoever hopes to minister with effectiveness and relevance in the opening years of this century must face the world head-on with reasoned, wise, biblical answers to a world that has lost its way. The warnings of the Scriptures are many and clear.

Is there an issue for which you have no answer? Find a Bible commentary or a theological book that addresses your concerns.

November 8

With the crisp winds of autumn stripping the trees of their colorful leaves, no one can ignore the similar changes in the cycle of life. But one thing doesn't change: God's faithfulness. He continues to meet needs as He answers prayer.

How has God modeled His faithfulness in your life through its many changes? Sing a praise song to Him for His faithfulness.

November 9

Only our God can strengthen the weak and reassure those who are growing at the same time. He specializes in doing the impossible, yet He still meets our deepest needs. What a mighty God we serve!

God is both great and personal.
Read Isaiah 40.

November 10

My prayer is that you will enjoy God's gracious blessings, which come to those who place their earthly treasure in His work. May our Lord wonderfully reward you for investing your treasure in eternal things . . . and may we never forget the importance of holding all things loosely.

Where is the treasure of your heart found?
Meditate on Matthew 6:19-21.

November 11

Even though we can't see the worldwide extension of the body of Christ, God has knitted our hearts together in a most unique way. I am relieved to know that visible presence is not a prerequisite for love and trust.

Though brothers and sisters in Christ, we each face differing levels of persecution. Pray for those members of the body who face adverse circumstances in Christ's name.

November 12

Time—that unstoppable, ever-pressing, never-resting river—refuses to be ignored for very long. But God always provides exactly what we need to complete what He expects. That's grace.

Are you worried that you will not complete your tasks on time? Relax. Read Matthew 6:24-34.

November 13

By today's standards, quantity seems more significant than quality. At least, that's the way it appears on the surface. But I'm willing to believe that most people still value character, values, and truth above cheap imitations that have no substance.

Cultivate a character of integrity and sincerity in your life. Model the characteristics of Philippians 2:3-4.

November 14

How is your spiritual inventory? To cover up for a sagging stock, you may do as most people—rearrange the display rather than restock the shelves. Spiritual window-dressing is always easier than in-depth restoration. A quick polish job does wonders for the surface, but it never lasts . . . not down deep, where it counts.

Want to restore your soul? Medititate on the words of Ephesians 5:1-2.

November 15

The biblical term God uses most often when referring to His affirmation is blessing. Because of overuse, unfortunately, that great word has lost some of its punch. Nevertheless, our Lord pours out His blessings on our behalf in endless demonstrations of grace, mercy, and peace. How blessed we are!

In what ways has God blessed your life — both in the large and small things? Thank Him for those blessings today.

November 16

As I write these words, I'm at thirty-eight thousand feet in a DC-10. Life gets simple up here. Deadlines and demands are temporarily put on hold. It's amazing how a little height can help us cope with the weights that so easily beset us.

It needn't always take an airplane to gain perspective. Spend some quiet minutes alone, and reflect on the areas that God is working in your life.

November 17

Remind yourself of His promises regarding generosity. Call to mind a few biblical principles that promise the benefits of sowing bountifully. Bumper crops, don't forget, are God's specialty.

What seeds are you sowing in your life? Where are you sowing them? For guaranteed growth, water them with the rich nutrients of God's Word and your prayers.

November 18

Spiritual defection wears many masks. A lowering of moral standards. A compromise of ethical excellence. A breakdown of integrity. What can be done? The spiritual antidote God prescribes to counteract defection is encouragement. We are commanded to use it "day after day." The results can be nothing short of miraculous.

The encouragement described in Hebrews 3:12–13 is a daily exercise. Make words of encouragement part of your daily routine.

November 19

Excellence—authentic, true, Christ-honoring excellence —is something to behold! Because we have become accustomed to mediocrity, we are all the more impressed when we encounter beautiful and unusual quality. It stands out.

The excellence we must model is described in Philippians 4:8. Think on these things as you drive to work, buy groceries, and listen to others.

November 20

Are you giving sufficient time and attention to those closest to you? Does your family know how deeply you love them and how strongly you are committed to them? Is your allotment of time demonstrating those things to them? If so, keep it up. If not, now is the time to begin anew.

Use your unique gifts to demonstrate love and concern for your family. What can you do for them that can be the work of none other?

November 21

Why is it that we can't have a ready-made Christian life?
Why can't we buy the fruit of God's Spirit somewhere?
We laugh at such a thought, knowing full well that the
elements necessary for a joyful Christian life can't be
packaged or bought. They must be grown and cultivated
in our own lives.

*The fruits of God's Spirit are listed in
Galatians 5:22-23. Where can you see these fruits
growing in your life?*

November 22

Call me dated or idealistic if you wish, but my passionate
plea is that we unearth and restore the virtue of character
in our lives. Character must lead the way if we hope to
walk securely.

*How would you define character? How does
God's Word define it?*

November 23

We were created in God's image. Like Him, we possess an inner spirit with which He can communicate and from which we can respond in worship, in songs of praise, and in unselfish acts of obedience.

Mutual communication occurs when we make time for it. Allot at least ten minutes each day for talking to God and listening to His response.

November 24

In times of grief, remember this: Though the sting of separation is painful, death's curse no longer has power over the Christian. In fact, death becomes the gateway to heaven.

Take time to mourn the loss of a loved one. Cry out to God in your grief, and allow the assurance of His love to comfort you.

November 25

After the miraculous feeding of the five thousand, the disciples turned around in astonishment when Christ calmed the sea. You'd think they would have known that God meets needs in abundance, but they didn't. How many times must the Lord supply our needs before we believe that He will do that always?

Reread Matthew 14:13-36. Do you find yourself responding like the disciples did to God's faithfulness?

November 26

Prayer isn't linked to a formula or a place, certain words or postures. Prayer is a child's cry of faith to His Father.

Prayer happens when we show up and start talking to God. Do this with your Father today — talk to Him like He is your best friend.

November 27

How much joy and growth do you experience when you're cut off from the Source? For your life to bloom and bear the fruit of the Spirit, you must cultivate your relationship with the Father. The flowers and harvest are evidence of His work in your life.

Reflect on His role as your life's Source.
How are you gaining sustenance from Him today?

November 28

Paul pursued Christlikeness with the discipline and persistence of a runner in the Greek games. Unlike many of his contemporaries, Paul did not claim to have attained spiritual maturity. He continued to push ahead, following the example of Christ Jesus. He was determined to let go of the past and press on toward the goal.

Consider Paul's perspective in Philippians 3:12-16.
Leave your past behind you as well, and press forward
with determination on the road ahead.

November 29

There's nothing wrong with intellect, intuition, instruments, or instincts—when they complement a heart set on trusting, hearing, and responding obediently to God.

Do you tend to lean on your emotions or your intellect? Neither is sufficient by itself, and both must be measured against the truth of God's Word.

November 30

Don't drag your load around—get a reliable handle. Your handle is Christ, and the truth found in His Word makes your load more manageable. The good news is that Christ never wears out. He is the same yesterday, today, and forever.

Are you making Christ your handle in everyday life? Where is this most evident?

December 1

My deepest desire is that people will not only come to Christ as Savior, but also adore and worship Him as Lord. When that occurs, life takes on new meaning. Purpose replaces futility. Excitement replaces boredom. Joy replaces despair. And when sin's fierce grip is overcome, melodies are released from the heart.

The Christmas season is a time for singing God's praise! Choose a favorite carol and let it be the theme song of your day.

December 2

At Christmastime, the unbeliever tries to fill the emptiness with meaningless substitutes. All the "hopes and fears of all the years" are buried beneath a flurry of activity and a longing for something more. But for the believer in Christ, Christmas is a season of hope based in the reality of Immanuel—God with us.

How is Christ walking with you today? Thank Him for being present and near to your heart.

December 3

We'll face winters in our spiritual pilgrimages. But just as Paul urged Timothy to "come before winter" (2 Timothy 4:21), the comfort of companionship, the warmth of an embrace, and the encouragement of a familiar voice can ease the chill of the wind.

Call a friend today. Share your love and a word of encouragement, and be blessed in return.

December 4

We need the reminder that life is not a marathon of monotonous misery to be endured, but is above its circumstances—an awesome, ever-changing adventure to be enjoyed. Christians don't have to take their cue from a world that has lost its way. To God's people, joy is always in season!

Turn to Philippians 3:20-21. Ask God to make your perspective like that of Paul's in this passage.

December 5

Christ became one of us so that we might become children of God. That simple truth brings fresh perspective in a day that has lost its purpose in a world that has lost its way.

Think of a Christmas tradition that had great meaning for you as a child. Find a child with whom you can share it, and pass on the heritage.

December 6

As idyllic as the holidays may be for some, they are the toughest time of the year for others. It's easy to forget that what brings some people joy and satisfaction brings heartache to others. In those times, God's Word becomes our most comforting companion. It bring rest and reassurance to hurting souls.

As you read God's Word today, ask Him to give you a verse or two to share with another who needs the hope those words can give.

December 7

The birth of Christ. For the first and only time in human history, the Lord, the Creator, the image of the invisible God lay as a helpless infant in the arms of His mother. Remarkable though it seems, Majesty was dependent. The mystery of it all is a wonder to behold.

Do you have a chance to stand under the night sky for just a few moments? Think of what the Christmas sky must have looked like so long ago.

December 8

No matter what your relationship is with your own dad or with your children, you need to know that, as a child of God, you have the irresistible attention of your heavenly Father. And it's all because of Christmas.

There are moments when we just want to crawl up into the lap of our Abba Father.
Make some time to be alone with Him today.

December 9

Where would Christmas be without music? All kinds of music! Frankly, we think the whole yuletide season would fall flat were it not for the songs and carols, the orchestrations and classical presentations. It is these melodies, woven together with traditions and memories, that embellish the lovely tapestry called Christmas.

Do you have a favorite Christmas carol?
Sing it out loud, and sing it unto the Lord.

December 10

Christmas can be the happiest time of year, but it can also be the loneliest. I'm glad to know that, no matter the season, Christ is more than able to penetrate the deepest of wounds, bringing healing and hope to broken lives.

On this second Sunday of Advent,
invite someone to share a meal with you.

December 11

We'll soon be rounding the bend of this year's road. Keep on trusting and obeying Him in the long haul. Paul's encouraging words apply to all who faithfully cross the finish line: "There is laid up for me the crown of righteousness, which the Lord, the righteous Judge, will award to me on that day" (2 Timothy 4:8).

A long prayer walk might be just the refreshment you need for this season. Bundle up, and pray as you go.

December 12

In remembrance of the greatest Gift, we in turn give gifts of love, appreciation, and support. Jesus' gift keeps on giving in the lives of those who receive it.

Is there someone you know who needs to hear why the Baby came? Find a quiet moment to share the real Christmas story.

December 13

When our hearts are focused on sharing Christ, we'll enjoy the Christmas season to its fullest. We'll know we are giving one hopeful gift everyone needs—one which many people, if they heard it, would love to receive.

Read Romans 10:12-15.
Pray by name for the missionaries you know.

December 14

This Christmas, let's not rush through the holidays, thoughtlessly singing some carols and hurriedly exchanging a few presents. Like the wise men of old, let's linger in His presence and offer Him our gifts of quietness and worship and devotion and love.

Schedule an uninterrupted time of worship.
Use the time to sing praises, read Luke 2, or
simply lose yourself in the wonder of it all.

December 15

We are not told to bring something tangible or to make a promise that will require an extensive sacrifice. Instead, the eighteenth-century Latin hymn holds out a three-fold invitation that anyone can fulfill: *Come, behold, adore.* Christ is Lord!

We often have to schedule time to adore Christ in our busy lives. Ensure that a time of worship and adoration are part of your holiday plans this year.

December 16

Come. Set aside whatever you are doing and return to that ancient scene, by now more familiar to Christians than any other place in history. There, in a dimly lit enclosure near an overcrowded inn, is a small, wooden feeding trough full of straw. We're to come to that quaint place, unhurried and full of silent wonder.

Set aside what distracts you today, and allow your mind to hear the Christmas story as if hearing it for the very first time.

December 17

Behold. On the surface, there is no difference between this particular Baby lying on the straw and any other Judean infant . . . but deep within, He is like none other. We're to stop everything else and behold Him who was "born the King of angels."

Read Luke 2:1-20 aloud.

December 18

Adore. A casual glance isn't enough. A curious gaze won't do either. The Babe in the manger was not sent simply to arouse attention or satisfy idle curiosity, but to bring us to our knees . . . to cause us to worship Him, to adore Him, Christ the Lord.

We're told that the shepherds hurried to Bethlehem to see the Baby (Luke 2:16). In what ways can you hurry to be with Jesus this season?

December 19

The Christmas story is woven together like fine needle-point, with one dominant theme: giving. God gave His Son to humanity, Christ gave up His heavenly position, the angels gave their glad tidings, the wise men gave their gifts. Everyone participates in the giving and, as a result, grace abounds to all.

To whom might you give grace today?
Be watching for a chance to give what can't be earned.

December 20

Christmas is upon us, and I've always felt there is no more beautiful season! God's Word became flesh nearly two thousands years ago to dwell among us. There's no better way to welcome Him this Christmas than by choosing to devote ourselves to His Word during the coming year.

Now is a good time to select a Scripture reading plan for the coming year. What would you like to study and learn about God in the next twelve months?

DECEMBER 21

Loneliness and darkness were washed away by His princely presence, His infant cries, His tender touch on the virgin's cheek. His birth calmed the raging storms within the human heart. Let us never forget—that is our reason for rejoicing at Christmastime.

John 10:10 tells why Jesus came: "I came that they may have life, and have it abundantly." Spend time praising Him for His presence on earth.

DECEMBER 22

He loves it when we celebrate His departure from heaven, His miraculous Incarnation, His coming to live among us. He also smiles when we share our joy with others the whole year through. The greatest gift we can give to others is the One who gave Himself to us.

There are those around us who have never met the Baby of Christmas. Look for a chance to share the true meaning of Christmas with another today.

December 23

Our annual return to the Babe in Bethlehem's manger has a way of simplifying life. We are able to see ourselves and assess our activities with greater objectivity. Time seems to slow down as our lives quietly pass in review.

What will you give to Jesus in this coming year?

December 24

Somewhere beyond the twinkling lights, red ribbons, and big bows, you and I long for the quietness Christmas can bring to our innermost being. We desire to return to the simplicity of the Babe in Bethlehem's manger, which, like a gentle whisper, reminds us of the real reason for celebrating.

Come stand by the manger. Look in on the
Baby lying there. Imagine the birth announcement
of the heavenly host. Rejoice!

December 25

The manger of Bethlehem cradled God's ultimate gift, born out of a Father's heart of love and wrapped in swaddling clothes. It reminds us, too, of Jesus' love for a dark and dying world.

The shadow of the Cross surely fell across the manger.
In a quiet moment this Christmas morning,
thank God for His plan of redemption.

December 26

The end of the year is an excellent time to search our hearts. Let me encourage you to do that before December runs its course. Take time to pray and to think about the ways your walk with Christ could be more consistent in the next year.

Set aside a time to pray through your plans for the
coming year. Are there God-inspired goals that you
can add to the list?

December 27

As the year draws to a close, are you reflecting on the past twelve months? At the beginning of the year, you were challenged to make this year spiritually significant. I hope it has been that for you.

List the spiritual milestones of your year. Allow some time for God to bring them to mind, and then thank Him for what He has done.

December 28

Look behind you at the road you've traveled. Can you see the steep grades and the level plateaus? Can you recall a few of the hairpin turns as well as the straight, clear highways of the past? I'm sure you'll agree with me that God's faithfulness has guided us through every mile, every turn, and every detour.

Read Psalm 27:1-6, and be encouraged by the fearless trust in God of which it speaks.

December 29

The end of the year is upon us. Even though we still have a challenging stretch of road ahead, pause to remember "all His benefits," as the psalmist did (Psalm 116:12), during these twelve months.

Read Psalm 116:12.
Begin a list of all the benefits He offers.
Allow some time — this may take awhile!

December 30

Finishing well is a real art. Better said, it's a learned discipline. And it's more than the goal achieved; it's the process taken along the way.

As you make plans and resolutions for the New Year,
bring each one before the scrutiny of the Lord
for His approval.

DECEMBER 31

I always love to turn the final page of my "old year" calendar, waving a fond farewell to December. It's not that those former months were so difficult . . . it's rather that I find the future so much more exciting.

A time of praise is in order! Gather your family and friends to give testimony, one to another, of God's faithfulness in the past year.

ORDERING INFORMATION

If you would like to order additional resources from Insight for Living, please contact the office that serves you.

United States and International locations:
Insight for Living
Post Office Box 69000
Anaheim, CA 92817-0900
1-800-772-8888, 24 hours a day, seven days a week
(714) 575-5000, 8:00 A.M. to 4:30 P.M., Pacific time,
Monday to Friday

Canada:
Insight for Living Ministries
Post Office Box 2510
Vancouver, BC, Canada V6B 3W7
1-800-663-7639, 24 hours a day, seven days a week
infocanada@insight.org

Australia:
Insight for Living, Inc.
20 Albert Street
Blackburn, VIC 3130, Australia
Toll-free 1800 772 888 or (03) 9877-4277, 8:30 A.M.
to 5:00 P.M., Monday to Friday
iflaus@insight.org

World Wide Web:
www.insight.org